ACKNOWLEDGE[...]

Hamble Valley Tourism would like to thank [...]
recipe to this book and those below for their [...]
to the production and research of: -
Stirring Traditions, Hamble Valley on [...]

Jonathan Roberts for his foreword; Venika Kingsland for her introduction
and recipes; Rose Elliot for her recipes and quotes; the following Local
History Societies and individuals who where involved in researching the
food in the area and supplying the photos and facts; Eastleigh and District
Local History Society, Botley and Curdridge History Society, Hound Local
History Society, Hamble Local History Society, Bishopstoke Local History
Society and Patrick Kirkby. The following pubs, restaurants, attractions,
producers and community groups for submitting a recipe: The Anglers,
The Victory Inn, Ye Olde White Hart, Hiltonbury Farmhouse, The Jolly
Sailor, The Horse and Jockey, the Concorde Club, Oyster Quay, Wickham
Vineyard, Botleigh Grange Hotel, Regginas, Botley Park Hotel, The Village
Tea Rooms, Bursledon Windmill, Botley Mills, Fruitwise, Pickwell Farm, A
& M Johnson, Honey & Hive Products, George Gale & Co Ltd, Bishopstoke
WI, Bursledon WI, Botley WI, Bursledon Village Hall, The Asian Elders,
Hamble Community Market and Jubilee Sailing Trust.

Hamble Valley would also like to thank Ray Wilson and the Eastleigh
College Catering Students: Tom Davies, Barry Wotherspoon, Sean
Patterson, Matt Etherington, Charlotte Hanks, Samantha Daglish, Claire
Dicks, Stacey Gray, Roy Pritchard and Kyle Vincent for testing some of the
recipes.

STIRRING TRADITIONS is sponsored by

The Hedge End, West End and Botley Local Area Committee.
Bursledon. Hamble and Hound Area Committee.

*"The recipe that is not shared with others will soon be forgotten,
but when it is shared, it will be enjoyed by future generations."*

- Unknown

Foreword

Over the centuries, at one time or another, the Hamble Valley has been famous for two kinds of food - fruit and shellfish – not immediately thought of as complimentary to each other. Oysters and strawberries? Clams and cherries? Winkles and plums? The combinations seem rather daunting.

In the early part of the 20th century the strawberry fields in the Botley and Hedge End area produced prodigious quantities of succulent, high quality *Fragaria ananassa,* the modern pineapple strawberry that we eat with sugar and cream. It's largely a folk-memory now, but picking would start at the beginning of June and last for a month, and families of pickers would be up before dawn, at 4 am, so that the first consignments could catch the 8 am 'Strawberry Specials' out of Botley station for early delivery to London's premier hotels and restaurants where Hamble Valley strawberries were held in such high esteem.

'Strawberry Special', Botley Station - 1907

STIRRING TRADITIONS

Pickers would be given four three-pound baskets at a time (often made by the inmates of Winchester Prison): one to hold and pick into, the other three tied to the waist. When all four were full, they were taken to a weighing and packing shed, and the picker would be given a disk, worth two pence (h'penny a basket): the same rate for children and adults. At the end of the day the disks would be counted and recorded, and, at the end of the week, redeemed: one highly-competitive 12-year-old girl is on record as having picked 30-shillings-worth by the first Friday (an astonishing 900 lbs of strawberries), and 3,000 lbs – 1,000 baskets - over the month.

The big, juicy pineapple strawberry that she filled her baskets with is, in fact, a modern creation, easily post-dating the Middle Ages. The Romans tried to domesticate the wild strawberry (the commonest species is *Fragaria vesca* which grows on woodland margins and which the French call *fraise de bois*) as early as 200 BC; but it stubbornly resisted attempts at enlargement, however good the growing conditions provided. The earliest mention of the wild strawberry in English is in a Saxon plant-list of the 10th century, and for centuries it seems to have been brought into cultivation in England as much for medicinal and ornamental reasons as for its fruit. The roots and leaves were considered astringent – good for diarrhoea – and the fruit was used as toothpaste for cleaning up discoloured teeth, and as a salve for sunburn. But its fruits were always small. The Creamy Strawberry, *Fragaria viridis*, with its yellowish fruits and the Hautbois Strawberry, *Fragaria moschata*, whose flower stems are carried high above its leaves – both species grow wild throughout much of Europe and Asia – were not much bigger: Denis Diderot, the French 18th-century encyclopaedist, once compared the smaller strawberries he was familiar with to 'the tips of wet-nurses' breasts'.

Early travellers across the North American plains in the 16th century recorded carpets of bright red strawberries, so thick that their horses' fetlocks seemed covered in blood. These were *virginiana*, Virginian strawberries. Specimens were brought back to the Old World, but early trials were disappointing, and fruiting occasional – it wasn't realised at first that you needed male and female plants growing beside each other to achieve pollination and fruiting. Sizes, too, remained disappointingly small.

Then, in 1714, a French engineer and spy called Amédée Frézier was lurking around the town of Concepción in Chile, mapping Spanish strong-points for his employer, Louis XIV of France. He stumbled across, in the sand-dunes, a strawberry-like plant he had never seen before; it had large, juicy fruits, red, yellow or white. It was the Pine or Sand Strawberry, *Fragaria chiloensis*, which grows wild all along Chile's coastline, in the dunes and up into the hills behind. Frézier potted up six plants for his voyage home to Marseilles. Five survived. He gave one away to the king's gardener in Paris, Antoine Jussieu, and grew the rest on in the area of Brest, his home town. By the 1750s it had been discovered in France – nobody is quite sure where and who by - that if you grew *chiloensis* and *virginiana* side-by-side, they readily hybridised to produce fertile, vigorous plants whose fruit combined the size and juiciness of *chiloenis* with the scarlet colour of *virginiana*. An extra bonus was a delicious, pineappley flavour. Thus the modern strawberry, *Fragaria ananassa*, was born; of New World parents, in an Old World birthplace.

Oysters and shellfish were once plentiful in the Hamble area, and highly prized for their size and quality. Old records prove that they were harvested as early as the 12th century, and, until the Reformation, the monks of the Benedictine Priory of St Andrew (now the parish of St Andrew the Apostle) used, every spring, to send 20,000 Hamble oysters to their brethren at Winchester to help them through Lent. But by the early 18th century fleets of oyster boats from the East Coast had worked the oyster-beds to virtual extinction, and those wild native oysters that remained were prone to infection with disease imported by American oyster-shells tossed overboard from transatlantic liners.

In the Civil War period, the village-gardens of the Hamble valley were famous for their little black cherries (called merries). Richard Cromwell, who had the governance of England briefly and unwillingly thrust upon him when his father died – he was first and foremost a countryman and farmer – liked to make a special annual trip to the valley with his wife for the merriefeasts, as they were called, when the cherries were ripe. In the early 19th century, before the coming of the railways, it was still the custom for local families to enjoy autumn-Sunday-afternoon outings to the cherry-orchards of Ram-Alley, near Chandler's Ford, and sample the merries there.

The cherries that grew at Chandlers Ford had their origins, long before historic time, in the mountain valleys and upland forests of Central Asia. The *Prunus* genus, of which they are members, spread out from there throughout the northern temperate regions of the world. Cherries were gathered by primitive man (stones from wild fruits have turned up in Neolithic - 5,000-BC - sites from Turkey to Portugal) and were probably first domesticated in the Greece/Asia Minor area in around 500 BC. The Romans loved eating them. The Roman General Lucullus, victorious in the Mithridatic wars in the 60s BC, is credited with having brought a superior cherry variety back to Rome from Asia Minor. A delightful wall-painting of a partridge eating cherries has survived at the Villa Poppaea at Oplontis, in the shadow of Vesuvius. The villa, and the painting, was buried by ash in the catastrophic volcanic eruption of 79 AD that also destroyed Pompeii, nowadays just a few stops away down the Naples metro.

Jonathan Roberts

Food writer and farmer from West Dorset and author of "Cabbages and Kings: the Origins of Fruit and Vegetables", published by Harper Collins in 2001. Jonathan has had features on the BBC Radio Food Programme, Radio Solent, Radio 4 and has contributed to articles in Country Life and Readers Digest.

Variety is the key to good health. The Okinawans (longest – lived people in the world) eat 206 different ingredients every year, 38 of them regularly. how many do you eat?

Rose Elliot

STIRRING TRADITIONS

Introduction

Intrigued by Jonathan Roberts opening remarks in the Foreword, I was reminded that traditionally gooseberries and mackerel made good companions during Maytime, later will not do, as the gooseberries need to be tart. So I experimented with some early tart cherries and found that they made a tasty accompanying sauce to fish pie.

During the 17th century when there were plentiful cherry trees in this area, fishing provided a living for many families along the river Hamble. According to Dorothy Hartley in *Food in England*, in those days damaged or broken fish in fish markets would be given away free and this mixed fish was baked in an earthenware pot well greased with dripping and a chopped onion or two. This was then covered with mashed potato baked again and served with slabs of bread with dripping and cups of scalding hot tea. I can imagine someone livening up the taste of the fish with sauces of one kind or another. Taking inspiration from this I have made a fish, potato and onion pie, which makes an agreeable alliance with the cherry sauce, mentioned above, (recipe in the main meals section).

Apart from cherries, strawberries and other epicurean delights, plums arrived with the Romans, although some varieties were introduced much later. Whilst researching material for my forthcoming book *Great British Cuisine*, I was sent a charming anecdote by Viscount Gage about the origins of the name 'greengage.' According to him the variety known as greengage (plum, *Prunus domestica*) "was introduced in to England by Sir William Gage from Belgium, where it was known as the 'Reine Claude' sometime during the 18th century at Hengrave Hall in Suffolk, where a branch of the Gage family established from about the mid 17th century till the late 19th century. It was afterwards introduced in the gardens at Firle Place in Sussex. At school, all

Gage boys, including myself, were nicknamed 'Plum' or some variety of, and this habit may well be continued."

Many varieties of plums are turned into prunes. Some are freestone and have a high sugar content, the best ones coming from Agen in France. Prunes, of course are well known for their laxative properties, as is prune juice. Prunes make good stuffing for turkey and chicken, and are excellent snacks stuffed with almond or marzipan.

The whole area around Hamble was densely wooded, chiefly oak, yew and sweet chestnut. In the autumn lorries used to come to gather the fallen chestnuts to take to town for sale. Chestnuts (*Castanea sativa*) have been in Europe and the British Isles since prehistory and have formed a part of our diet for a very long time. Ancient Greeks such as Dioscrides and Galen complained about its flatulent qualities whilst hailing its medicinal properties, which allegedly protected one against certain poisons and the bite of mad dogs.

It is a pity that chestnuts fell out of favour appearing in the markets only at Christmas. They contain important amounts of trace minerals and are the only nut to contain significant amounts of vitamin C. Dried chestnuts used to be extremely valuable when we did not have refrigerators during the winter months. Pound for pound dried chestnuts contain 371 calories as compared to potatoes with only 86, and whole wheat at 240.

We have nothing like the number of chestnuts trees we used to have. This is probably because chestnuts seldom grow spontaneously, and when they were cut down they were seldom replanted. As they take something like fifteen years to mature and their yield is not optimal until they are fifty years old, people seldom planted them for their own enjoyment. As the saying goes 'the olive tree of your forefather, chestnut tree of your father, only the mulberry tree is yours.'(Brunetton-Governatori, A (1984) Le pain de bois, Toulouse.)

Although cheap and at one time plentiful, like many other foods of the past they are now a luxury appearing only at Christmas as an expensive delicacy for the few. It is worth remembering though that they are very versatile and can be used in both savoury and sweet dishes. I love the smell of roast chestnuts in London in the winter months. They go well with beef and lamb and also make a good stuffing for poultry. They are particularly nice as sweetmeats and in chocolate. Chestnut purée is often an ingredient in ice cream. Nesselrode Ice Cream, invented by M. Mouy for the Russian diplomat Count Nesselrode, is a mixture of chestnut purée, raisins, cherries, orange peel and sweet sherry mixed with ice cream and served with whipped cream and marron glacés. A recipe for a 'no-cook' chestnut and chocolate cake has specially been created for this book and is included in the desserts section.

Finally, Hamble Valley Tourism is to be commended for producing this cookery book. Throughout the Valley there is plethora of traditional tea rooms, pubs and some excellent restaurants offering good food and speciality dishes. Alternatively, picnics and barbecues can be enjoyed at the many country parks in the 800 acres of unspoilt countryside. Hamble Valley is also full of local producers where the freshest of ingredients, many of which are used in the recipes featured in this book, can be obtained. We trust that this book will whet your appetite and time and again *"you'll come back feeling you've discovered one of Britain's best kept secrets"* (Bath Chronicle).

Venika Kingsland

Venika Kingsland is a published author and has written on a variety of subjects. Recent publications include "A guide to Customs and Etiquette in India," "An Introduction to Hinduism" both published by Global Books. She is a major contributor to the 'Cultural Diversity Guide' published by ITV in 2003. Venika lives locally and is Hampshire Chronicle's cookery expert, contributing to articles on food and original recipes every week. She is also a Governor of Sparsholt College and a Board Member of the National Probation Service Hampshire.

Hamble Produce Market
during the
Hamble Valley
Food and Drink Festival

STIRRING TRADITIONS

Contents

CONTENTS

CONTENTS

Cakes and Bakes

The County Cheese Market was established in 1852 and was held on the third Thursday of every month. Great quantities of cheese were sold in the spacious square enclosure; the market was situated adjunct to Bishopstoke station on the west side of the Itchen Navigation at Barton in the South Stoneham Parish.

Alongside the station, was a square enclosed with rows of sheds and lines of rails, which extended along the fronts of the sheds. Other agricultural produce might be sold there, with a cattle market being established here in 1876 by Messrs. Hunt and Bance.

Courtesy of Hampshire Records Office

TOP98/2/7

Broccoli Cream Cheese Soup

225g head of broccoli
25g butter
1 medium onion, chopped
2 leeks, whites only, chopped into rings
2 tablespoons fine oatmeal
1pint (600ml) milk
1pint (600ml) vegetable stock
175g low fat cream cheese
Salt and pepper to taste

Wash broccoli, detach florets and chop stalks. Melt the butter in a pan. Add chopped onions, leeks and broccoli stalks, sweat for 10 minutes over a low heat.

Stir in the oatmeal; add the milk and stock and season. Simmer for a further 10 minutes, then turn off heat and leave the soup to cool.

In a separate pan, steam the florets for 4 minutes and reserve.

Add the cream cheese to the cooled soup and liquidize. Adjust seasoning at this stage if necessary.

Return soup to the pan and gently heat through, do not allow it to boil.

Serve in individual bowls with the broccoli florets floated on the top.

Bishopstoke Womens Institute

There are around 450 beekeepers in Hampshire varying from the small producer with a couple of hives at the bottom of the garden to those who run upwards of 300 colonies. Honey contains natural sugars, traces of pollen and has its own antiseptic properties. Hayfever sufferers take local honey as the pollens in it help to build their immunity to the hayfever. It must be local honey with the local pollens in it. Honey was also used in the First World War due to its antiseptic properties.

Salade de Carottes Râpees (Grated Carrot Salad)

Serves 4 - 6

750g (1½ lbs) carrots
2 tablespoons chopped parsley
1 – 2 tablespoons snipped chives
6 tablespoons honey dressing (as below)

Peel and grate the carrots finely, place them in a bowl with the chives and parsley. Pour over the dressing and toss well.

Transfer the salad to a serving dish and chill lightly before serving if preferred.

Honey Dressing

6 fl oz (175 ml) olive oil
2 fl oz (60ml) white wine vinegar
1 teaspoon mustard powder
1 clove of garlic, peeled and crushed
1 teaspoon clear honey
Sea salt and freshly ground black pepper, to season

Put all the ingredients in a screw top jar, adding salt and pepper to taste.
Shake well. Refrigerate until required

If the honey is set, heat briefly in the microwave to loosen, this will prevent the dressing from becoming lumpy.

Makes 8 fl oz (250ml)

Alan & Margaret Johnson, Honey and Hive Products,
Grasmead, Limekiln Lane, Dean, Bishops Waltham
Tel: 01489 892390

Onion Bhajees

8 oz (225g) gram flour
1 tablespoon rice flour
1 tablespoon sesame seeds
1 tablespoon dhania-jeera powder
(coriander and cumin powder)
2 teaspoons chilli powder
¼ tablespoon turmeric
1 tablespoon salt
2 large onions, cut in half and chopped finely
1 tablespoon finely chopped fresh coriander
7 fl oz (210ml) water
Oil for deep-frying

Sieve gram flour into a large bowl then mix in all of the remaining dry ingredients together with the coriander and onion. Gradually add the water, mixing thoroughly until a thick batter is formed and the onions are well coated.

In a wok, karhai or deep fat frying pan, heat the oil to a depth of 2 - 3inch over a medium heat. When it is the correct temperature a drop of batter will rise immediately to the surface without turning brown.

Drop heaped teaspoons of the onion batter into the oil (take care not to make the bhajee too large otherwise the centre will not cook). Fry a few at a time, turning if necessary, for about 5 - 6 minutes until golden brown. Repeat until all of the bhajees are cooked allowing time for the oil to reheat between each batch.

Drain on absorbent paper.

Eastleigh Asian Elders

Vegetable Pakoras

Use the same basic recipe but also adding a variety of chopped vegetables e.g. cauliflower, aubergine, potato and peas, potato and spinach, etc. You may need to add more flour if the vegetables are more moist, but aim for the same batter consistency.

Eastleigh Asian Elders

Chestnut Soup

12 oz (350g) chestnuts, peeled
2 pints (1.2 litres) vegetable stock
Salt and pepper

Place the chestnuts in a saucepan and cover with the stock. Bring to the boil and gently simmer until the chestnuts are soft. Drain off the liquid and retain it. Purée the chestnuts.

Return the stock to the saucepan and add the chestnut purée stirring well. Season with a little salt and pepper, reheat and serve.

An old traditional Hampshire recipe

The Victorian Kitchen at
Manor Farm

Manor Farm has a vegetable patch that is worked by the
Victorian characters 'Walter Stubbs' and 'Bert Deable', who
plan and maintain it to provide an authentic recreation of a
Victorian cottage garden. Old 'Victorian' varieties of fruit and
vegetables are grown, rather than more modern varieties, to
maintain authenticity. The garden provides a valuable
educational resource as well as a picturesque and attractive
feature. The produce is used by the interpreters in the
farmhouse ('Mrs Earwicker' et al) to demonstrate cooking,
and on most Sundays it is used to provide a meal at
lunchtime for the farm staff and volunteer 'characters'.

Stilton Pâté

Serves 4

8 oz (225g) Stilton, mashed
2 oz (50g) unsalted butter
2 tablespoons brandy
2 tablespoons single or double cream
A few walnut halves to garnish

Mash the ingredients together thoroughly or process them, then press into a suitable dish and refrigerate. Turn out and top with a few walnut halves.

Serve with Melba toast.

As an alternative add chives or parsley to the mixture

Mrs Earwicker, Manor Farm
Manor Farm Country Park, Pylands Lane, Burseldon,
01489 787055

I am convinced that eating lots of fruit and vegetables is the key to vibrant health and the more you eat, the more you get to like them. Organic ones are wonderful if you can get them, but ANY fruit and vegetables are good news.

Rose Elliot

Vegetable Soup

4 oz (115g) pearl barley
4 oz (115g) lentils   } *or 12 oz (350g)*
4 oz (115g) yellow split peas   *mixed broth mix*
3 pints (1.8 litres) of water
2 Knorr vegetable cubes
2 carrots
1 small swede
1 parsnip
1 onion
1 leek
1 head of Curly Kale, about 5 leaves

In a large pan cover the pearl barley, lentils and split peas with water and soak overnight. The following day, drain any remaining liquid from the soaked mix.

Add 3 pints of water and the crumbled vegetable cubes to the broth mix. Prepare and then dice the vegetables, add to the broth. Mix thoroughly, cover the pan with a lid and simmer the soup gently for 1 hour.

May Draper, Pickwell Farm
Pickwell Farm, Portsmouth/Grange Road, Netley
023 8040 4616

In the early 19th century, watercress was a staple diet of the working classes and was most often used for breakfast in a sandwich. If they were a poor family and could not afford bread then watercress would just be eaten on its own, which is why it has become known as 'poor man's bread'. Watercress began to be grown commercially in the chalk streams of Hampshire and Dorset, and was then taken by train to Covent Garden for sale in 'loose' form, from stalls, in the famous market alongside flowers and newspapers.

Covent Garden Market in the 19th century

Cream of Watercress Soup

400g watercress   Serves 6
50g butter
50g onion, sliced
50g leeks, sliced
1 whole carrot, peeled and sliced
750ml chicken stock
250ml single cream
100g cubed potatoes
Salt and pepper

Wash the watercress well and drain thoroughly.

In a large saucepan melt the butter over a low heat, stir in watercress, onion, leek and sliced carrot. Cover with lid and cook for 2 minutes. Add chicken stock, cream and cubed potatoes. Simmer for a further 15 minutes, then allow to cool.

Transfer to a blender, blend until smooth.

Reheat the soup gently without boiling, seasoning with salt and pepper to taste, and then serve.

As an addition to the soup, fry off some diced bread in clarified butter until crisp and golden. Garnish the soup with the croûtons and a whirl of cream

David Ophaus, The Concorde Club & Moldy Fig Wine Bar
The Concorde Club & Hotel, Stoneham Lane, Eastleigh
Tel: 023 8065 1478

The Whyte Harte Inn is one of the oldest pubs in Hamble, being built around 1563, although some of its timbers are taken from ships' hulls that date back to 1400. A window featured in the bar is one of the oldest existing windows, and is listed with English Heritage. The gargoyles that are incorporated into the bar were once part of Netley Abbey. It is said that a tunnel runs from under the pub to the waterfront which was used by many a smuggler – if you look inside the fireplace you can still see the door!

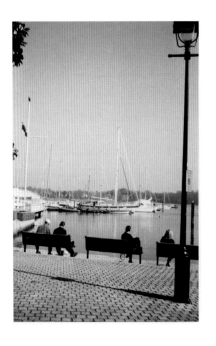

Views of Hamble

Bantry Bay Mussel Broth

2 oz (50g) onion
2 oz (50g) carrot
2 oz (50g) celery
2 oz (50g) butternut squash or pumpkin
2 oz (50g) leek
4 oz (115g) potato
2 cloves of garlic
2 oz (50g) unsalted butter
2 oz (50g) pearl barley
2 pints (1.2 litres) fish or chicken stock
6 oz (175g) mashed potato
36 clean and bearded mussels
¼ pint (150ml) double cream
2 fl oz (50ml) Jamesons whiskey
1 level teaspoon milled black pepper
1 oz (25g) chopped chives

Finely dice the vegetables into ¼ inch cubes and cook in butter for 3 – 4 minutes on a medium heat. Mince the garlic and add to the vegetables and cook for a further 2 minutes stirring occasionally, add black pepper and cook for 1 minute, add pearl barley and stock and cook until the pearl barley is soft. Thicken the stock with the mashed potato and then add the mussels. Cook until the mussels are open (3 – 4 minutes if fresh, longer if frozen), discarding any that do not open, finally adding the cream and whiskey. Do not allow to boil.

Garnish with chopped chives and serve with warm white soda bread.

G.K Monquay, Ye Olde Whyte Harte,
Ye Olde Whyte Harte, High Street, Hamble.
Tel: 023 8045 2108

Char-Grilled Sea Bass with Noodles and Wilted Spinach and Crushed Cashew Nut Salad.

Serves 4

4 Sea Bass, whole
400g, fine noodles
500g spinach, washed and shredded
200ml white wine vinegar
2 tablespoons Dijon mustard
400ml olive oil
50g dill, finely chopped
200g cashew nuts, unsalted
8 tablespoons olive oil
Parsley, to garnish

Wash, clean and trim the sea bass and refrigerate until needed. Place noodles in a pan and cover with boiling water and boil for 5 minutes, and then simmer for a further 15 – 20 minutes.

To wilt the spinach, boil at least 2 pints of water in a large pan add a pinch of salt and the shredded spinach, leave for 4 – 5 minutes, before draining thoroughly.

Meanwhile, mix the white wine vinegar, mustard, 400ml olive oil and dill together to form the salad dressing. Also, toast the cashew nuts in a dry frying pan then crush them lightly.

Reserve a little of the dressing for garnish, before adding the remainder together with the crushed toasted cashews to the drained spinach, mix together.

Heat a griddle pan; brush the fish with the remaining olive oil and char-grill.

To serve:

Drain and rinse the noodles in hot water and toss in olive oil. Place the noodles on a plate/bowl; lightly pile the spinach salad on the noodles and then the grilled fish. Drizzle the reserved dressing round the plate and garnish with a sprig of parsley.

Eastleigh College Catering Students

In the late Middle Ages beer was considered a staple food and was regulated by the civil authorities. The craft of beer brewing had been introduced into England in the early 1400's by the Flemish Dutch, when it replaced ale as the staple drink. Ale was an unstable produce, tending to sour easily and it did not travel well. It was produced by individual households as a cottage industry. Beer on the other hand with its use of hops was stronger and did not go off easily, but required an industrial process to produce it. Beer became a wholesale trade and Tipplers or Tapsters undertook its retail. The brewing and sale of beer was identified in some quarters with a moral decline which led to people neglecting their work in favour or playing unlawful games, such as dice and cards in beer houses. Therefore in the 16th century licensing laws were introduced into the country.

Coconut and GB Beer Batter Prawns

Coconut and GB Beer Batter Prawns

Seasoning
1 teaspoon cayenne pepper
½ teaspoon each of salt, paprika and ground black pepper
¼ teaspoon garlic powder
1 teaspoon each of onion powder, dried thyme, oregano
2 oz (50g) flour

Batter
½ pt (300ml) Gales GB beer
6 oz (175g) flour
2 eggs
1 teaspoon baking powder
6 oz (175g) grated coconut (best blitzed very fine in a blender)
Uncooked tiger prawns (tail fan on if possible), peeled and de-veined
Oil for frying

In a bowl, mix all the seasoning ingredients together.

In a separate bowl, mix the baking powder, eggs and beer together with the flour until a smooth batter is formed.

Place the coconut in a further separate bowl.

Dip each prawn into the seasoning mix and shake off the excess, then dip into the batter again waiting for the excess to drip off. Coat each prawn in the coconut and place on a baking sheet.

Heat the oil in a deep fat fryer and drop each prawn in carefully holding the tail fan. Cook for 2 – 3 minutes. Drain on paper towels. Serve immediately.

Jon Daley, Gales Brewery

In 1861 the Itchen, from all accounts, teemed with trout that were stated to have averaged 18 – 20 oz each. These were the palmy days of the Itchen, but since then the river has greatly deteriorated.

The Anglers in Bishopstoke in 1900

Fish Bake

12 oz (350g) cod fillet
12 oz (350g) smoked haddock
6 oz (175g) prawns
6 oz (175g) mussel "meats"
4 oz (115g) onion
1 pint (600ml) milk
3 oz (80g) butter
2 oz (50g) flour
1 teaspoon English mustard
1 oz (25g) parsley, chopped
4 oz (115g) cheese
1 lb (450g) potatoes

> For an extra touch
> Add 100ml cream

Preheat the oven to 220ºC/425ºF/Mark 7

In a large pan gently sauté the chopped onions in 1oz (25g) butter until soft. Add the milk and gently simmer. Add the cod and haddock and simmer for approx 4 – 5 minutes. Remove fish when cooled.

Make a white sauce with remaining butter and the flour using the fish flavoured milk. Add the mustard, 2oz cheese and chopped parsley and season to taste. Flake the fish into the sauce and add the cooked prawns and mussels.

Put the ingredients into a prepared ovenproof dish. Cook and mash the potatoes and carefully cover the fish. Sprinkle with the remaining cheese and place in the oven for 20 minutes.

Garnish with a lemon wedge and serve with a crisp side salad.

Martin Lazarski, The Anglers Inn
The Anglers Inn, 17 Riverside, Bishopstoke.
Tel 023 8061 2995

Mixed Fish Pie with Cherry Sauce

1 large red onion, diced
25g butter
500g short crust pastry
1 large cold baked potato, diced with skin on
500ml Béchamel sauce or
Can of condensed mushroom soup
Good dash of Tabasco sauce
Salt and pepper to taste
500g mixed fish, including mussels, prawn, smoked salmon, trout, mackerel, cooked
500g puff pastry
Beaten egg for brushing pastry

Preheat the oven 200ºC/400ºF/Mark 6.

Grease and line a 30 x 20cm rectangular ovenproof dish with the short crust pastry.

Fry the onion in the butter until it is soft. Add the potato and the Béchamel sauce or mushroom soup, Tabasco and salt and pepper, stir over the heat for two minutes. Mix and then add the fish.

Pour the fish mixture into the prepared dish and cover with the rolled out puff pastry. Press the two pastries together, using your fingers to crimp the edges together. Make a couple of tiny slits in the top to allow the steam to escape. Brush with beaten egg and bake in the preheated oven for 30 minutes or until golden.

Serve with Cherry Sauce.

Venika Kingsland

Cherry Sauce for Fish Pie

450g tart cherries
30g butter
1 tablespoon flour
Salt and pepper to taste
Good pinch of nutmeg

Stone the cherries and put them in a pan with half the butter and just enough water to cover them. Cook until they are soft. They may either be left as they are or put through a fine sieve. Heat the remaining butter in a saucepan, add the flour and stir until it is absorbed in the butter. Pour in the cherries and add salt, pepper and the nutmeg. A little sugar may be added if the cherries are too tart or some lemon juice if too sweet. Bring to the boil and serve hot.

Venika Kingsland

Many mounds of oyster shells are to be found in the banks of the River Hamble, as oysters were once plentiful in the area. Old records show they were harvested in the 12th century and the Hamble area .was renowned for the quality and quantity of its oysters. Indeed, each mid – lent from 1292, according to the archives, the monks of Benedictine Priory of St. Andrew (now the parish of St Andrew the Apostle) sent 20,000 of them to their brethren in Winchester. In return the six monks at Hamble received 21 loaves and 42 flagons of ale weekly.

Up to 1710 large fleets of oyster boats from the East coast and beyond would visit the Hamble for the season. However by this time the beds were almost completely dredged out and no oysters were left. It was nearly 100 years before oysters returned in any remarkable quantities.

Many of the oyster boats would be moored at Badman Creek unloading their catch and waiting for a favourable tide to return to their home ports.

Thai Spiced Oriental Tiger Prawn, Salmon and Fresh Oyster, with Tagliatelle Verde

4 tablespoons extra virgin olive oil
1 white onion, finely chopped
1 clove of garlic, puréed
1 fresh red chilli, finely chopped
300g salmon fillet, chopped into 2cm cubes
12 oysters, freshly shelled
12 tiger prawns, cooked and peeled
500g fresh tagliatelle verde, cooked al dente
50g coriander, roughly chopped
4 tablespoons soy sauce
Salt and pepper, to season
50g coriander, picked for garnish

Serves 4

Heat a large wok and add the olive oil. Add the chopped onion, garlic and red chilli and sweat off until onion is transparent in colour. Add the diced salmon and whole oysters and cook for 2 – 3 minutes. Then add the prawns, cooked tagliatelle and the chopped coriander, and mix all of the ingredients gently, season with salt and pepper as necessary. Drizzle the soy sauce evenly over the contents of the wok.

Serve in shallow bowls and garnish with the picked coriander.

For a finishing touch, drizzle with a little olive oil to add shine

Elliot Steel & Graham Mosely, Oyster Quay
Oyster Quay, Mercury Yacht Harbour, Satchell Lane, Hamble
Tel: 023 8045 7220

R.V. HOSPITAL. NETLEY.
AERIEL PHOTOGRAPH. TAKEN FROM SUPERMARINE FOUR SEATER
CHANNEL TYPE FLYING BOAT.

Royal Victoria Country Park, a Hampshire County Council Countryside Service Site was the home of Netley Hospital from 1863 to 1978. In the 1860's an Officers Mess was built to accommodate male army officers working at the hospital as well as medical students. Many formal dinners were held in the mess with regimental silver being used and officers wearing formal mess kit.

For the patients in the hospital in the 1890's breakfast was at 7.30am, dinner at 12.30pm and tea at 5.30pm. Diets varied for each patient and included grilled chop, grilled steak, soup, chicken and beef tea.

Curried Chicken

3 lb (1.5 kg.) chicken
2 fl oz (50ml) oil
4 oz (115g) onions
1 oz (25g) curry powder
1½ oz (40g) apple
1½ oz (40g) mango chutney
¾ oz (20g) tomato purée
½ oz (15g) desiccated coconut
1 small bouquet garni
¾ pint (450ml) chicken stock
Salt

Serves 4

Preheat the oven to 180ºC/350ºF/Mark 4

Cut the chicken as for sauté, heat the oil in a suitable pan, season and fry the chicken to a light golden brown, remove from the heat and keep warm.

Peel and finely chop the onions, fry in a little oil without colouring them, add the curry powder and cook slowly for 3 – 4 minutes.

Peel, core and chop the apple, chop the chutney and mix with the apple. Add the tomato purée, apple and chutney, coconut, bouquet garni and chicken to the pan and stir in the stock. Bring to the boil, season as required and set to cook in the oven for 45 minutes.

Remove bouquet garni, skim off any fat, adjust the seasoning and consistency and serve with plain boiled rice.

Courtesy of the Army School of Catering, St Omar

MAIN COURSE – **MEAT and POULTRY**

One of the traditions of the Army is that curry is served at least once a week and after formal events such as reunions and church services. Historically, the strong spices in curry had the advantage of concealing the disagreeable flavour of rotting meat that was often served in the British-officered Indian Army in the 19th century, also linked to the presence of the British Raj in India. Army personnel and civil servants acquired a taste for spicy food whilst in India and brought their newly found dishes home (or to other parts of the Empire) with them.

From about 1960 both Army and Navy male and female officers lived in the mess, which finally closed with a formal dinner and fireworks in 1978.

Chicken Mozzarella Melts

4 chicken breasts
2 tablespoons red pesto
A small tub of cherry tomatoes
Grated mozzarella cheese
Olive oil

Serves 4

Flatten the chicken breasts with a meat hammer and gently pan fry until golden brown in a little olive oil and cooked throughout. Take them out of the pan and spread each one with ½ tablespoon of the red pesto. Next, slice the cherry tomatoes in half and place on top of the chicken. Lastly sprinkle the grated mozzarella on top and gently grill until the cheese has melted.

Serve with salad leaves and crusty bread for a quick and easy mid- week supper

Arthur Price, The Victory Inn
The Victory Inn, High Street, Hamble.
Tel: 023 8045 3105

The Victory is named after the HMS Victory, a first rate warship in the time of Admiral Nelson, the ship had over 100 guns and around 800 officers and men. In 1806 HMS Victory was refitted, which coincidentally is the same date on The Victory Inn's builders mark – IC1806.

Chilli Chicken Nest

4 chicken breasts, not skinned
225g breadcrumbs   Serves 4
4 cloves of garlic, finely diced
3 teaspoons paprika
1 red chilli, deseeded and chopped
1 green chilli, deseeded and chopped
2 teaspoons fresh basil, finely chopped
2 teaspoons fresh parsley, finely chopped
1 egg, beaten
1 tablespoon olive oil
500g potatoes
1 egg yolk
50g butter
1 teaspoon chilli powder
2 teaspoons mixed herbs
100ml milk
2 shallots, finely chopped
1 teaspoon chicken bouillon
¾ pint (450ml) water
½ pint (300ml) red wine
Salt and pepper
Freshly chopped parsley, for garnish

Using a filleting knife, gently release ⅔ of the skin from each chicken breast. Mix the breadcrumbs, garlic, paprika, chopped chillies and fresh herbs together in a bowl, then bind with the beaten egg. Season with salt and pepper. Carefully spoon approximately 3 tablespoons of the stuffing under the skin of each chicken breast; the skin should be able to completely cover the mixture.

Preheat the oven to 200ºC/400ºF/Mark 6

Heat the olive oil in a sauté pan, add the stuffed chicken breasts one at a time and seal by cooking on both sides for 2 – 3 minutes, being careful not to dislodge the stuffing. Transfer into a roasting tray and cook in the oven for about 25 minutes.

Peel and boil the potatoes. Then rice or sieve them together in a bowl adding the egg yolk, butter, chilli powder, mixed herbs and milk, beat until smooth. Season to taste and place the mixture into a piping bag with a star nozzle, and pipe 4 nests.

Melt the butter in a saucepan and gently sweat the shallots off, amalgamate the water with the chicken bouillon, add to the saucepan and bring to the boil. Add the wine lower the heat to a simmer and allow to reduce by half.

To finish, remove the chicken from the oven, keep warm and allow to rest for 5 minutes. Grill the potato nests for approximately 5 minutes until golden brown. Season and adjust the consistency of the sauce if necessary.

To serve, place the chicken at a 45º angle against the potato nest and drizzle the sauce over the chicken and nest and around the plate, sprinkle with parsley.

Eastleigh College Catering Students

EASTLEIGH
C O L L E G E

Hiltonbury Farm was probably one of the earliest of the many farms that were built in the late 16th and early 17th century belonging to Hursley Park Estates and the Manor of North Stoneham, the original building appearing on a map of 1588. The distinctive chimneys are a Victorian addition, and these and other features are repeated on a number of buildings that were owned by Hursley Park Estates at this time. In 1638, Richard Major, a son of the Mayor of Southampton, acquired the Great Lodge of Hursley Park, and the accompanying Hursley Estates. In 1649, his daughter, Dorothy, married Richard Cromwell, third but eldest surviving son of Oliver Cromwell, and the young couple lived with Dorothy's father at Hursley.

In the 1890's Hiltonbury Farm was sold to Cranbury Park Estates, and remained in their ownership until it ceased to be a working farm in the late 1970's. The farmhouse remains as a public house, in the centre of the North Miller's Dale housing development, built on what had previously been the farmland.

Corned Beef Hash

200g corned beef (2 x 100g tins)
200g cooked potatoes
1 onion, finely chopped
1 tablespoon horseradish
Salt and pepper
A little oil

Serves 6

Chop the corned beef and cooked potatoes into bite sized pieces.

Lightly fry the finely chopped onion in the oil until transparent and cooked through. Mix together all the ingredients, season as necessary and transfer into an oven - proof dish and brown under the grill.

Serve with a poached or fried egg, baked beans, peas or fresh vegetables.

Lynne Sinker. Hiltonbury Farmhouse
Hiltonbury Farmhouse, North Millers Dale, Chandlers Ford,
Tel: 023 8026 9974

The Horse and Jockey is situated in Curdridge, near to Botley. Botley was once well known for its amount of public houses. Up until 1798 horse, carriage and coach traffic had to use a ford to cross the River Hamble, and due to it being tidal, all traffic often had to wait for the tide to drop. This often meant having to wait for up to 6 hours in the small town. Due to this increase in visitors Botley became home to 14 public houses.

The Horse and Jockey, Curdridge, 1903,
courtesy of Botley & Curdridge Local History Society

Botley was home to Edwards Brewery, which was housed in a wooden building situated behind the present Brewery Bar Public House in Winchester Street. Trade Directories for Botley show that the Brewery was in existence in 1852 when it was owned by John Edwards who was listed as a Brewer and Beer Retailer.

Horse and Jockey Lamb with a Herb Crust and Redcurrant Jus

4 bone rack of lamb
1 oz (25g) Hampshire honey
2 oz (50g) fresh breadcrumbs
1 oz (25g) chopped fresh mixed herbs
Squeeze lemon juice
Salt and pepper
Gales redcurrant wine
¼ oz (5g) butter, for sauce

Preheat the oven to 200ºC/400ºF/Mark 6

Have the butcher French Trim the rack of lamb and remove any fat for you.

Mix the remaining ingredients and apply as a crust to outside of meat. Place the prepared lamb in an ovenproof pan.

Roast in a medium/hot oven until cooked to your liking. Remove lamb from oven, add redcurrant wine to pan juices and reduce.

Carve lamb and arrange on plate, whisk a little butter into sauce and pour over lamb.

Serve with a selection of fresh vegetables and potatoes

Jon Daley, Gales Brewery
Horse and Jockey, Curdridge, Botley
Tel: 01489 782654

Lamb, Leek and Mango Pies

Serves 4

500g lean lamb, diced, preferably boned leg
25g butter
100g onions, diced
1 clove of garlic, finely chopped (optional)
25g flour
500ml beef stock
2 bay leaves
500g defrosted puff pastry
1 egg, well beaten
2 ripe mangoes, yellow/red when ripe
100g large leeks, diced
Pinch salt and pepper

Preheat the oven to 180ºC/350ºF/Mark 4

Fry off the lamb in a heavy bottomed pan with the butter over a moderate heat. Add onions and if using garlic, stir until the meat is browned all over. Add the flour, mix well, continue to mix until flour turns slightly brown then add the warm stock, stir gently until the flour is dissolved. Add the bay leaves and simmer for approximately ¾ hour until the meat is tender. Some water may need to be added if the mixture becomes too thick during cooking.

Meanwhile, roll out the puff pastry to an ⅛ inch thickness. Cut into 6 rounds using 5inch (13cm) fluted cutter. Egg wash, bake in medium oven until golden brown, remove and leave to one side.

Cut the mango down side of flat stone, skin and chop. Fry prepared mango and leeks off in a little butter, drain then add to the lamb mixture.

To Serve:

Split the pastries in half horizontally. Using a perforated spoon to avoid too much liquid, equally distribute the mixture on the cut surface of each pastry "bottom" half. Add liquid as required, place pastry tops over the lamb mixture to form enclosed pies.

Garnish with fresh herbs and serve

David Ophaus, The Concorde Club & Moldy Fig Wine Bar
The Concorde Club & Hotel, Stoneham Lane, Eastleigh
Tel: 023 8065 1478

Quick and Easy Pheasant, see page 51

The Concorde Club was previously a Church of England school that was opened on the 10th January 1876 with 75 mixed pupils. John Humphrey Jones was master and his wife, Sarah Jane, the needlework mistress. It was soon realised that a gallery was needed for the infants to observe the lessons and that a fence to the school playground was necessary. For disciplinary reasons boys and girls were separated in 1881 by alterations to the classrooms.

North Stoneham School at the turn of the 19th century

Photograph from 'The Book of Stonehams'
(published by Halsgrove, Tiverton, Devon)

Quick and Easy Braised Pheasant with Bacon and Cranberries

50g clarified butter
2 pheasants, each cut into 4 pieces
100g back bacon, diced
50g red onions, sliced
100g button mushrooms
½ pint (300ml) red wine
½ pint (300ml) water
1 clove of garlic, chopped
100g cranberry sauce
Salt and pepper

Serves 4

Preheat the oven to 200ºC/400ºF/Mark 6

On the hob, melt the butter in a casserole dish over a moderate heat, add the 8 pieces of pheasant, and seal on both sides until brown, remove from pan.

Add all the other ingredients, and bring to boil, then reduce to a simmer for 5 minutes, add the browned pheasant pieces, cover with lid and braise in the oven for approx 1½ hours until the pheasant is tender.

At the end of the cooking time, return the casserole to the hob, remove pheasant from liquid and keep warm. Remove any excess surface fat from the sauce and then boil vigorously to reduce by half.

Arrange pheasant pieces onto a plate, mask with sauce and serve.

David Ophaus, The Concorde Club & Moldy Fig Wine Bar
The Concorde Club & Hotel, Stoneham Lane, Eastleigh.
Tel: 023 8065 1478

The Jolly Sailor in Old Bursledon is located on the banks of the River Hamble. It was built in 1713, has been a pub since 1845 and is a Grade II Listed building. It was on this site during medieval times, that England's men-of-war were launched. Edward III himself came to witness the St George take to the water on April 23rd, 1338.

Shipbuilding at Bursledon reached its zenith during the Napoleonic wars when the toll on English woodlands was fearsome, - a single 64-gun ship required no fewer than 3,070 cartloads of oak and other timbers.

By courtesy of Bursledon Village Hall

The Jolly Sailor's reputation is widespread, greatly enhanced in the 1980's when it featured prominently in the highly popular BBC TV series "Howard's Way".

STIRRING TRADITIONS

Moroccan Lamb

1 kg. lamb steak   Serves 4
500g red onions, chopped
1 tablespoon olive oil
*2 tablespoons each of cumin, ground coriander, mixed
herbs and mint*
A good pinch of salt and pepper
*1 teaspoon each of garlic, chilli powder, nutmeg, cinnamon
and cloves (use fresh nutmeg if possible)*
2 tablespoons paprika
400ml dry white wine
1 tablespoon of lamb bouillon (or if unobtainable, beef)
200g sultanas
200g chopped dried apricots
2 x 500g tins chopped tomatoes

Cut the lamb into about 1¼ inch cubes (or ask your butcher
to do this for you), place the diced lamb and olive oil in a
large heavy bottomed pan and brown over a medium heat,
and then add the sliced red onions. Add all the other
flavourings and the chopped tomatoes. Bring to the boil,
reduce heat and simmer or oven bake at
180ºC/350ºF/Mark 4 for about 1½ hours or until the meat
is tender.

Add the sultanas and chopped apricots and adjust the
seasoning to taste.

A fantastic flavoured dish with lots of different and exciting
flavours. Great with lots of fresh vegetables or a good crisp
salad.

Adrian Jenkins, The Jolly Sailor
The Jolly Sailor, Lands End Road, Old Bursledon.
Tel: 023 8040 5557

Char–grilled Beef Tournedos, Rosti potato, Red Wine Jus, split with Garlic and Parsley Butter

*175g (6oz) fillet steak
3 round shallots
Duck fat or olive oil, to confit
150g small cut Provencal vegetables (peppers, aubergines, courgette and garlic)
1 tablespoon tomato purée
1 large potato
50ml red wine jus
10g garlic and parsley butter, melted
1 tomato, for concasse
3 sprigs of chervil, for garnish
Oil for cooking
Salt and pepper, to season*

Cook the vegetables before hand by frying in a little oil and tomato purée, dash of jus, salt and pepper until just cooked.

Place shallots into saucepan and put in duck fat or olive oil and slow cook and simmer until soft for about 15 – 20 minutes and simmer and then take off the stove.

Grate the potato and rinse under water to remove the starch, drain thoroughly in kitchen paper and season with salt and pepper.

Warm a frying pan or galette with a little oil and place a 6 cm (2½ inch) metal pasty cutter into the pan and add the grated potato until it is about 3cm (1inch) deep, and pan fry until golden then turn and repeat, place in the oven to finish.

To make the tomato concasse, score the top of the tomato with an X, place in boiling water for 10 seconds, remove and place in ice-cold water, this releases the skin. Peel off the skin and cut into 4, remove the seeds, pat dry on a kitchen towel and then cut into 5cm squares.
Melt parsley butter and warm the jus.

To arrange:

Place the 3 shallots around the outside.

Place Provencal vegetables in the centre of the plate using a cutter to shape them, remove cutter, carefully place rosti on the vegetable stack and then place the fillet on top of the rosti.

Put the tomato concasse into the warmed jus. Then drizzle over the steak at the last minute, spoon the melted garlic and parsley butter around the stack, place the sprigs of chervil on the shallots and serve.

Botleigh Grange Hotel
Hedge End, Southampton.
Tel: 01489 787700

Botleigh Grange

Botleigh Grange was purchased sometime between 1868 - 1869 by Mr Thomas Hellyar Foord, he was a man of the most abstemious habits and up to a few years before his death never had but two meals a day, breakfast at 8am and dinner at 4pm and under no circumstances could he be persuaded to take refreshment in between these times. He attributed his splendid health and long life principally to this, coupled with regular walking and exercise.

Despite this Thomas Hellyar Foord ensured that his guests dined sumptuously, but they had to do so alone as he did not join them.

Char-grilled Beef Tournedos, see page 54

Hampshire Sausages

Serves 4

8 large pork sausages
1 large onion, sliced
3 medium eating apples
300ml cider
Small quantity of water
Salt and pepper to taste

Place the water in a heavy frying pan over a medium heat. Add the sausages and cook them in the water and their own fat until almost cooked through. Add the onions at this stage and fry them with the sausages.

Core and slice the apples, leaving the peel on. When the onion is transparent add the apple to the frying pan and cook for a further 2 minutes stirring frequently. Add the cider and cook until the liquid has reduced to a sauce and the apples softened. If using sparkling cider add this very carefully bit by bit as the liquid will froth up in the pan. Season with salt and pepper and serve with mashed potatoes and a glass of cider.

As a variation, add herbs, sage would be ideal, at the same time as the cider. This recipe can also be used with pork chops.

Stephen and Julia Hayes
Fruitwise

During 1937 I can remember having a meal at Eastleigh County High school for 2d, for which you had tomato soup followed by banana custard.

Gordon Cox, Eastleigh & District LHS

The Home Tavern on the corner of Leigh Road and Station Hill was built in the 19th century. It began as a brew-house where ales were made and sold for church revenue. These were known as church ales. With changing times and requirements the brew-house often became the village inn. The ancient brew-house then became 'The Old House At Home' which was built in 1712. This was a thatched building, which was demolished in 1887. However certain parts of the original building were incorporated in the new structure.

The Dining Room, Sisters Quarters, Netley Hospital

Spring Thyme Chicken

With pan-fried new potatoes, courgettes, carrots and green beans tossed in minted butter

1 chicken supreme
1 spring onion, chopped
Ball of buffalo mozzarella cheese
Salt, pepper
White wine
1 courgette
1 whole carrot
A few green beans
½ block of butter
New potatoes
Sprig of thyme, for garnish
Mint and Parsley, chopped for garnish

Serves 1

Preheat the oven to 170ºC/325ºF/Mark 3

Make an incision in the chicken breast and stuff with the spring onions and mozzarella cheese. Season with salt and pepper, put in a suitable size dish with a little bit of white wine drizzled over the top of the chicken and place in oven for 15 – 20 minutes.

Top and tail the carrot and courgette, cut them both in half and then "turn" them, place them in salted boiling water until cooked, cook the green beans separately. Cook the new potatoes, drain and toss in butter. When the vegetables are cooked toss in butter with the chopped mint,

To serve, place the vegetables neatly on a plate with the new potatoes and finally the chicken, garnish with a sprig of thyme and chopped parsley.

Dean Hutson, Holiday Inn,
Holiday Inn, Leigh Road, Eastleigh
Tel: 0870 400 9075

Hamble Valley Venison with White Beans and Bacon

4 venison steaks, from the loin/ haunch and preferably Roe
1 onion, finely sliced
80g pancetta, cut into lardons
20g butter
10ml olive oil
2 cloves of garlic, crushed
200g white beans, soaked overnight and drained
750ml chicken stock
4 tomatoes, skinned, deseeded and chopped
50g flat leaf parsley, picked
Oil for brushing

Serves 4

For the sauce:

10 juniper berries
100ml port
50g onion, diced
50g carrot, diced
50g celery, diced
1litre venison or beef stock (fresh preferably)
1 sprig of thyme
5g butter

To cook the Beans

Sweat the sliced onions and pancetta in the oil and butter over a moderate heat until just beginning to colour.

Add the garlic and the drained beans and stir well for 2 minutes, add the chicken stock and bring to the boil. Reduce heat to a very gentle simmer and cook until beans are tender, about 1 hour.

Drain and keep the stock that is left and reduce to a syrup. Stir this into the beans. Just before serving, stir in the parsley and tomatoes into the bean mixture and season.

For the sauce

In a saucepan fry the onion, carrot and celery until golden brown, about 10 minutes.

In a separate pan dry toast the juniper berries until they begin to sizzle and the aroma is released. Add the sprig of thyme and the toasted juniper berries to the browned vegetables and de-glaze with the port, reduce to a syrup. Add the stock, simmer to reduce again, skimming any impurities as you go. The sauce should be reduced by ¾, finish by whisking a knob of butter in.

To cook the Venison

Heat a frying/sauté pan until very hot with no oil in for at least 5 minutes. Brush the steaks with a little oil and sear for 1 minute on each side. When browned add a large knob of butter and reduce the heat to medium. Cook for 2 more minutes on each side.

Remove, keep warm and allow to rest for 5 minutes, and then serve with the reheated beans and sauce.

James Graham, Head Chef,
The Restaurant at Wickham Vineyard
Wickham Vineyard, Botley Road, Shedfield.
Tel: 01329 834042

Wickham Vineyard was established in 1984 with a first planting of 6 acres and has since been extended to 18 acres. It is one of the larger commercial vineyards in England producing between 30,000 and 50,000 bottles per annum. The site used to be a strawberry field but was ideal as a vineyard as well because it is a south-facing slope. This means the grapes receive as much sunlight as possible and are also partially protected from frost, which tends to roll down the hill. One problem facing the original owners when they established the vineyard was that it is on a clay base. This is very good from a nutrition point of view for the grapes but not good for drainage. Therefore a wide network of land drains was installed throughout the vineyard to ensure the vines do not get "wet feet". The vineyard now grows a variety of white and red grapes including the famous Pinot Noir which does very well in a cool climate.

Farmers Pastry

1 lb (450g) shortcrust pastry
8 oz (225g) minced rump steak
1 large onion, finely chopped
2 medium potatoes, finely chopped
½ small swede
Salt and pepper, to season
1 lb (450g) Bramley apples, peeled
2 oz sugar
1 egg, beaten for glaze

Makes 4
pastries

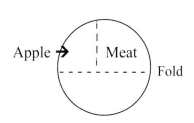

Preheat the oven to 220ºC/425ºF/Mark 7

Roll out pastry to ¼ inch thick. Cut 4 rounds the size of a dinner plate. Keep 4 other pieces of pastry aside to use later to divide the sweet section of the pastry from the meat side.

Mix meat, onion, potatoes, swede and salt and pepper together. Slice apples and put in a separate bowl with the sugar.

Take one of the pastry rounds and in the top half put ¼ of the meat mixture so that it occupies two thirds across the width, as shown in the diagram. Press out a spare piece of pastry to make a barrier, then put the apple mix onto the other third of the pastry width.

Dampen edges and fold up as the lower half of the round over the filled section to form a pasty shape. Glaze with egg wash and put into the preheated oven for 25 minutes then reduce temperature to a moderate heat 180ºC/350ºF/Mark 4 and cook for a further 45 minutes.

Mrs Earwicker, Manor Farm
Manor Farm Country Park, Pylands Lane, Burseldon,
01489 787055

The building that houses Regginas was built in the 17th century. Prior to becoming a restaurant, it housed 3 generations of the Bailey family who were builders and undertakers. When the Market Hall was built next door in 1848, the Baileys were employed as maintenance contractors. Arthur Bailey continued the business as an ironmonger until his death in the 1960's.

Arthur Bailey's Shop in High Street, Botley,
Courtesy of Botley & Curdridge Local History Society

Vitello Vesuvio
Escalopes of bread-crumbed veal
on a bed of Spaghetti Arrabiata

1 tablespoon olive oil　　　　　　　Serves 2
Small onions, chopped
2 cloves of garlic, chopped
1 red chilli, chopped
400g tin chopped tomatoes
2 escalopes of veal
2 tablespoons flour
I egg, beaten
80g (3oz) breadcrumbs
250g dried spaghetti

For the Arrabiata sauce

Put olive oil in a pan with finely chopped onions, garlic and chilli and slowly fry off. Add the tomato and simmer for ten minutes.

For the Veal

Meanwhile, beat the veal escalopes until they are thin; coat them in the flour and then dip them into the egg and then into the breadcrumbs.

Fry the veal in a little olive oil until golden brown.

Cook the spaghetti and add the tomato sauce

To serve, place cooked spaghetti on plate with veal on top

David Hall, Regginas
Regginas Restaurant, 13 High Street, Botley.
Tel: 01489 782068

Lentil Dal

Dal is easy to make and a great way o
adding protein and interest to a simple
plate of vegetables and/or grain.

250g split red lentils
1 large onion, peeled and chopped
1 bay leaf
½ teaspoon turmeric powder
1 tablespoon grated fresh ginger
850ml water
2 teaspoons ground cumin
2 teaspoons ground coriander
3 cloves of garlic, peeled and crushed
Juice of 1 lemon
Salt and freshly ground black pepper

Serves 4

Put the lentils into a large saucepan with the onion, bay
leaf, turmeric, ginger and water. Bring to the boil and
simmer for 20 minutes, until the lentils are tender and pale.
Remove and discard the bay leaf.

Put the cumin and coriander into a small saucepan and stir
over the heat for a few seconds, until they smell aromatic
and gorgeous, and then stir them into the dal.

Add the garlic and lemon juice to the dal and season with
salt and pepper.

Serve with brown basmati rice.

*Three most magical ingredients are fresh ginger, turmeric
and garlic. They're therapeutic as well as tasty. Use them
all together in a dal or add them to curries and stir fries.*

Rose Elliot

Little Gem, Chicory and Watercress Salad with Mustardy Vinaigrette

2 Little Gem lettuces   Serves 2 - 4
2 chicory
Bunch or packet of watercress
1 teaspoon Dijon mustard
½ clove of garlic, crushed
1 tablespoon red wine or cider vinegar
3 tablespoons olive oil

Cut the little Gems into thick wedges – sixths or eighths, right down through their stems; remove outer leaves from the chicory, then cut the hearts into quarters or eighths. If you are using bunched watercress, which is great if you can get it, remove the thickest part of the stems.

Wash all the leaves and shake dry, then heap them up on a serving dish or put them into a salad bowl.

For the dressing: put the mustard, crushed garlic, vinegar and a little salt into a bowl and mix with a fork or small whisk, then gradually whisk in the oil. Season to taste.

Just before serving the salad, drizzle the dressing over and around the salad, and grind some more pepper coarsely over the top.

Fresh herbs are magical. Not only do they transform simple foods, but they add their own nutritive and therapeutic qualities. Try adding thyme to your dishes when you've got a sore throat, or fresh rosemary when you want to feel energized. -   Rose Elliot

Baby Spinach and Summer Berry Salad

When my friend Annie raved about this salad she'd eaten in Vancouver, I though 'yeah right...' But she kept on about it so I tried it. She was right. It's a really unusual yet delicious mixture. Rose Elliot

1 tablespoon raspberry vinegar
2 tablespoons olive oil   Serves 2 - 4
Salt and freshly ground black pepper
1 red onion, finely sliced
100g flaked almonds
225g firm log of goats cheese
1 packet baby leaf spinach
225g summer berries: raspberries, strawberries or blueberries

Mix the raspberry vinegar, olive oil and some salt and pepper in a salad bowl. Add the onion, mix and leave on one side. This can be done in advance if convenient – this allows the onion to soften in the dressing but isn't essential.

Put the flaked almonds into a dry saucepan, sit over a low heat for a few minutes until they turn golden then tip them onto a plate before they overcook.

Cut the goats cheese into bite-sized pieces, put into a grill pan and put under a hot grill until nicely browned.

Mix the spinach, berries and almonds into the salad bowl; top with the hot goats cheese and serve at once

Rose Elliot

Look at the meal as a whole: 'naughty but nice' foods like chips can be more guilt free if you eat them with a big leafy green salad.

Rose Elliot

If using sparkling cider in this recipe, add slowly to avoid it "frothing" up.

Apple and Cider Braised Cabbage

This dish is an ideal accompaniment to roasted or grilled meat

1 Savoy cabbage, heart only
1 large onion, finely chopped
50g butter
2 eating apples (Red Pippin or Cox can be used)
250ml (1 cup) cider

Take the Savoy cabbage and slice it into pieces about 1cm by 5cm. In a saucepan, fry the onion in the butter over a moderate heat until soft and golden, then stir in the cabbage. Peel and core the 2 apples then cut into small pieces and add to the saucepan. Stir in the cider, cover and reduce the heat and simmer gently for 10 minutes, stirring occasionally.

Stephen & Julia Hayes, Fruitwise

Manor Farm was once at the centre of the rural settlement of Botley. It gradually became more isolated as, with the building of the turnpike road in the 19th century, the village that we know today grew up a mile to the north. The antiquity of the farm is reflected in the farmhouse, the earliest part of which dates from medieval times. The domestic fire used for heating and cooking in the original 15th century open hall can still be seen to this day. The various barns and outbuildings that surround the farmyard are all of historical significance, the oldest dating from the 16th century. Over the centuries the farmhouse has undergone extensive development as successive owners improved the accommodation in line with their needs and their available wealth. In 1984 the farm was opened to the public.

The Farmhouse

Super Duper Cheese Dish

4 oz (115g) cooked macaroni
1 cauliflower, cooked
6 eggs, hard boiled
1½ pints (900ml) cheese sauce
4 oz (115g) cheese
4 tomatoes, sliced

Preheat the oven to 220ºC/425ºF/Mark 7

Put macaroni in large ovenproof dish and cover with one third of the cheese sauce. Put a layer of cauliflower on top and cover with one third of cheese sauce. Place halved eggs on top and cover with the remainder of the sauce. Sprinkle with cheese and arrange sliced tomatoes on top. Put in hot oven for approximately 30 minutes until really heated through and cheese is melted and browned.

Serve with peas and crusty bread.

Mrs Earwicker, Manor Farm
Manor Farm Country Park, Pylands Lane, Burseldon,
Tel: 01489 787055

Cheese Fritters

This is an all time favourite children's dish – and grown ups love it too!

600ml (1 pint) milk or soya milk
1 small onion, peeled and stuck with 1 clove
1 bay leaf
125g semolina
125g vegetarian Cheddar cheese, grated
1 teaspoon mustard powder
Salt and freshly ground pepper
1 large egg, beaten with 1 tablespoon of water
Dried breadcrumbs for coating
Oil for shallow frying

Serves 4 - 6

Bring the milk, onion and bay leaf to the boil in a large saucepan. Remove from the heat, cover and leave to infuse for 10 – 15 minutes.

Remove and discard the onion and bay leaf. Return the milk to the boil, gradually sprinkle the semolina over the top, stirring all the time. Simmer for about 5 minutes, stirring often, to cook the semolina, then remove from the heat and beat in the cheese, mustard and some salt and pepper to taste.

Spread the mixture to a depth of about 1 cm on an oiled plate or baking sheet. Smooth the surface and allow to cool completely.

Cut the mixture into squares of triangles. Dip each shape first into the beaten egg, then dried breadcrumbs, to coat thoroughly. Shallow fry in hot oil until crisp on both sides, then drain the fritters well on kitchen paper.

Serve immediately, with lemon wedges.

Rose Elliot

Watercress Sauce
for Mackerel, Trout or Nut Roast

200g watercress
300ml water or fish stock
25g butter
25g flour
Salt to taste
Tablespoon of cream

Remove all the stalks from the watercress, this may seem a laborious process but the results justify the extra work. Simmer the stalks in the water or fish stock until they are tender. Drain, discard the stalks and set aside. In the meantime chop the remaining watercress very finely. Heat the butter and cook the flour in it until it turns creamy. Add the stock, chopped watercress and a little salt. Stir and bring to the boil, remove from the heat and add the cream before serving.

It is excellent served with hot smoked mackerel, grilled trout or nut roast and buttered boiled potatoes.

Venika Kingsland

Beer has also played a part in the history of another of Hamble Valley's villages, Fair Oak. The name of this village derived from a fair that was held in the Village Square near the oak tree on 9th June every year. The first person to erect his stall at the fair had to call at the front door of the Old George Inn (seen on the right hand side of the photo) to collect the 'key' of the fair. He then returned it to the landlord at the back door and received a quantity of beer, thought to be a gallon.

The fair was discontinued after the First World War and all that remains of the original oak tree is a chair made from its wood in Winchester Cathedral.

Fair Oak Village Square in the 1800's, showing the oak tree and the Old George Inn

Prize Old Ale Salad Dressing

5 tablespoons olive oil
½ onion, finely chopped
1 clove of garlic, chopped
½ bottle Prize Old Ale, drink the rest!
3 tablespoons white wine vinegar
2 teaspoons Hampshire honey
2 tablespoons whole grain mustard
Salt and pepper

Heat 3 tablespoons of olive oil over a medium heat in a pan, add the onions and garlic and sauté until soft. Add the prize Old Ale, vinegar and honey and reduce for 4 or 5 minutes. Set aside to cool.

Place the cooled mixture in a blender with the mustard and seasoning. With the motor running add the remaining oil.

Jon Daley, Gales Brewery

Kitty on the Hamble

The River at Bishopstoke - 1912

STIRRING TRADITIONS

Ginger and Butternut Squash Risotto

2 tablespoons olive oil
850g butternut squash, halved, deseeded, peeled and cubed
4 medium leeks, washed and sliced
2½cm piece of root ginger, peeled and chopped
2 cloves of garlic, chopped
375g risotto rice
1 litre hot vegetable stock
Salt and freshly ground pepper to taste
3 – 4 tablespoons freshly chopped coriander
Parmesan

Heat the oil over a medium heat, add the squash, leeks, ginger and garlic and cook for about 8 minutes stirring frequently.

Stir in the rice, then add the stock a ladle at a time ensuring all the liquid has been absorbed before adding the next, this takes about 20 minutes. Stir frequently.

Season the risotto and stir in the coriander and serve with freshly grated Parmesan.

Jubilee Sailing Trust

DESSERTS and PUDDINGS

In 1939 the WRVS used the lower room in Bursledon Village Hall as a services canteen, where the troops were very appreciative of tea from teapots as contrasted with the brew which they had from urns in their various billets. However, the disposal of tea- leaves through the buildings doubtful drains was not really desirable, so the tea leaves were thrown out of one of the low windows at the back, where the land sloped steeply. One day, forgetting this whilst making a swift departure, one of the helpers climbed out of the window and landed ankle deep on a morass of tea leaves!!

William Cobbett the radical writer, who lived in Botley, would not have agreed with the troops drinking tea!

'I view the tea drinking as a destroyer of health, an enfeebler of the frame, an engenderer of effeminacy and laziness, a debaucher of youth, and a maker of misery for old age.' Cottage Economy By William Cobbett

This picture is of Bursledon Church Hall, taken on 9th April 1924 for the wedding of Charles Norton and Ruth Fisher

Tartes des Pommes Marianna

Shortcrust pastry to line flan tin
60g butter
90g caster sugar
1 egg, beaten
1 lemon
1 large cooking apple, grated or chopped
60g raisins

> Squeeze the juice out to ensure that there is not too much moisture

Preheat oven to 190ºC/375ºF/Mark 5 and line an 8inch flan tin with prepared pastry.

Over a low heat, gently melt the butter, add the sugar, grated lemon zest, juice of half the lemon, beaten egg, chopped or grated apple and raisins. Mix together and put in the prepared flan tin.

Bake until set for 30 – 45 minutes

Bursledon Womens Institute
Bursledon Village Hall

Photo: Kevin Kingsland

Mucky Mud Dip

8 oz (225g) chocolate
1 oz (25g) butter, diced
2 tablespoons warm water
Marshmallows, pineapple chunks, banana, orange
segments, or small cubes of cake, for dipping

Gently melt the chocolate and butter together with the 2 tablespoons of warm water. (Either in the microwave or over a bain-marie). Keep it warm. Dip your chosen fruit or cake into the melted chocolate and allow to set.

Mrs Earwicker, Manor Farm
Manor Farm Country Park, Pylands Lane, Burseldon
Tel: 01489 787055

STIRRING TRADITIONS

Strawberry Valley Pavlova

3 medium eggs, separated
225g caster sugar
1 tablespoon cornflower
1 teaspoon vanilla essence
1 teaspoon white wine vinegar
Double/ whipping cream
Strawberries to decorate

Prepare moderate oven, 180ºC/350ºF/Mark 4.

Mark a 20cm circle on non-stick baking parchment, placed on a baking sheet.

Place egg whites in a grease-free bowl and beat until stiff but not dry. Mix together sugar and cornflour and add to the beaten egg whites a little at a time whisking well after each addition. Whisk in the vanilla essence and the vinegar.

Spoon or pipe the mixture into the circle marked on the parchment covered baking tray.

Put into the oven and immediately and reduce the heat to 140ºC 275ºF/Mark 1. Bake for 40 minutes. At the end of the cooking time, turn the oven off and leave the meringue to cool in the oven without opening the door for at least 1 hour.

When cold decorate with freshly whipped cream and Hampshire strawberries.

Bishopstoke Womens Institute

DESSERTS and PUDDINGS

The house at Shamblehurst Manor was owned in 1547, the last year of Henry VIII's reign, by the Marquis of Winchester, William Paulet, who was one of Henry's courtiers. The Paulet family lived at Basing House but owned much property in the Southampton area including Shamblehurst Manor and Netley Abbey.

The house is a cross passage design where the access was via a passage which ran across the building behind the main fireplace. The house seems to have had a quiet existence being occupied by Paulet retainers and operating as a large farm. In the early part of the 20th century the farm was a major strawberry producer.

Strawberry Picking

STIRRING TRADITIONS

This is a delicious summer dessert and a simple way of serving strawberries in a spectacular style.

Strawberry Open Tart

8 oz (225g) plain flour
2½ oz (70g) icing sugar
1lb (450g) strawberries
5 oz (150g) butter
1 egg
8 oz (225g) redcurrant jelly

Preheat oven to 180ºC/350ºF/Mark 4.

Sift flour into a large bowl. Make a well in the centre and add the butter, icing sugar and egg. Gradually work the mixture together with your hands adding the flour bit by bit. Alternatively mix all the pastry ingredients together in a food processor. Chill pastry in refrigerator for at least 30 minutes.

Push pastry into the base and side of a 10inch (25cm) loose-bottom flan tin. Prick the base all over with a fork. Bake for 20 minutes. Remove from the oven and allow the pastry case to cool before removing from tin.

Slice strawberries and arrange in the case. Melt redcurrant jelly in a saucepan, bring to boil and reduce to a syrup. Pour over fruit and chill.

Jenny Schwausch,
Strawberry Cottage & Hedge End Womens Institute

Between 1806 and 1820 Botley was the home of the famous journalist and radical politician, William Cobbett, who described the village as the most delightful in the world. There is a memorial stone to William Cobbett in the village square.

'Botley is the most delightful village in the world, it has everything in a village that I love, and none of the things I hate.'

Thus wrote William Cobbett, author of Rural Rides, who farmed in Botley for 13 years from 1806.

'Every woman, high or low, ought to know how to make bread. If she do not, she is unworthy of trust and confidence: and, indeed, a mere burden upon the community'

Cobbetts Country Book, By Richard Ingrams.
David & Charles (Holdings) Ltd, Vermont, USA

'When we came down to Botley, we there found the turnips as good as I had ever seen them in my life, as far [as] I could judge from the time I had to look at them. Mr. Warner has as fine turnip fields as I ever saw him have, Swedish turnips and white also'.

Rural Rides, Cobbett

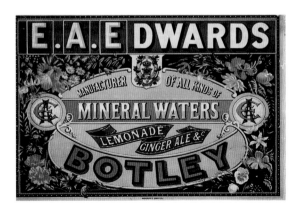

STIRRING TRADITIONS

Sticky Toffee Pudding and Butterscotch Sauce

2½ litres water
300g chopped dates
3kg. granulated sugar
1½kg. plain flour
28g baking powder
14 medium eggs, beaten
1¼kg. unsalted butter
50g icing sugar
¾ litre of double cream

Serves 20

Preheat the oven to 200ºC/400ºF/Mark 6.

In a large pan heat the water with the dates and sugar over a medium heat, bring to the boil, remove from the heat and allow to cool. In a separate bowl mix together the remaining dry ingredients, with the exception of the icing sugar, add to the saucepan. Add the beaten eggs and stir well.

Put the mixture in a lined 10inch square tray and cook for about 1 hour 15 minutes. Remove from the oven and leave to cool.

To make the butterscotch sauce, reduce the butter and icing sugar together over a medium heat until the temperature reaches 120ºC. Whisk in the cream.

Serve the portions of pudding with a good helping of butterscotch sauce and possibly clotted cream.

Chris Taylor, Executive Head Chef
Botley Park Hotel and Country Club,
Winchester Road, Boorley Green, Botley
Tel:01489 789242

Hikers Delight

8 oz (225g) rolled oats
4 oz (115g) ground almonds
4 oz (115g) caster sugar
6 oz (175g) melted butter
2 eggs

Preheat oven to 150°C/300°F/ Mark 2

Mix dry ingredients together, fold in beaten eggs and melted butter. Spread mixture in a shallow 11 x 7 inch (28 x 18cm) tin. Bake in a slow oven until golden brown for approximately 30 minutes. Cut whilst still warm.

Gooseberry Meringue

> *Botley is the starting point or the Strawberry Trail so when you have made your biscuits, you can follow the strawberr waymarks for an 8 mile stroll down to Netley.*

1½ lbs (750g) gooseberries
2 tablespoons water
2 tablespoons white sugar
3 egg whites
4 oz (115g) light brown sugar

Put gooseberries in a pan with the water and cook them until soft. Then add the white sugar and spoon into ovenproof dish.

Whisk egg whites until stiff, whisk in half the brown sugar, fold in remaining sugar and spread over the gooseberries. Place in oven, 180°C /350°F/Mark 4 for 20 minutes, until meringue is brown on top. Serve warm or cold.

May Draper, Pickwell Farm
Pickwell Farm, Portsmouth/Grange Road, Netley,
Tel: 023 8040 4616

Strawberry and Passion Fruit Meringue Roulade

For the Meringue

Serves 6

6 egg whites
150g caster sugar
Few drops of vanilla essence
1 teaspoon cornflour

For the filling

4 passion fruits, squeezed
150g strawberries
300ml (½ pint) double cream, whipped
Icing sugar, redcurrants and mint to garnish

Whisk egg whites to a stiff peak; add the sugar, vanilla essence, sprinkle over the cornflour and continue to mix.

Spoon mixture onto a medium size baking tray approx 9 x 12 inch (23 x 30cm) using parchment paper to avoid the meringue sticking and level off.

Bake for 1 hour in a cool oven 150ºC/300ºF/Mark 2, remove and allow to cool.

Turn meringue out onto a piece of cling film. Spread the whipped cream over the meringue; add squeezed passion fruit and strawberries leaving some for the garnish.

Gently roll up, remove the cling film and place on to a serving plate. Garnish with remaining strawberries, redcurrants, sprig of mint and a generous dusting of icing sugar.

David Ophaus, The Concorde Club & Moldy Fig Wine Bar
The Concorde Club & Hotel, Stoneham Lane, Eastleigh
Tel: 023 8065 1478

Strawberry Delight

1 tub low fat cream cheese
2 tubs strawberry fruit corner yoghurts
12 inch (30cm) sponge flan case
1 pot double cream
1 punnet fresh strawberries

Mix the cream cheese and yoghurt together until well blended, then spread the mixture over the sponge flan case.

Whip up the double cream and pipe into swirls around the edge of the flan.

Decorate with fresh strawberries

Chris Pullen, Village Tea Rooms.
Village Tea Rooms, High Street, Hamble,
Tel: 023 8045 5583

The Tea Rooms date back to the late 18th century and once housed a Coffin Makers and Rope Makers. There is an air raid shelter in the garden with chimney drains which run from the house to the outside toilet. During some excavations 2 toilets were discovered which were probably the original public toilets in the Square as the houses on the opposite side of the road didn't have any!

The country all around is very beautiful, and attracts many local artists, as well as parties of cyclists who go to Hamble to get a 'crab tea'.

Extract from: The Captain, vol VI, October to March 1902.

Dark Chocolate Terrine with Orange Custard

4 egg yolks
600ml double cream
3 oranges
2 tablespoons Grand Marnier
1kg. dark chocolate
1 litre double cream
200ml egg yolks
125g granulated sugar
1 tablespoon brandy

Serves 12

Prepare a crème anglaise, in a saucepan warm the 600 ml of cream, put the 4 egg yolks in a separate bowl then slowly add the warmed cream, whisking all the time. Return to the saucepan and heat gently, stirring all the time, until the mixture coats the back of a spoon, do not allow to boil at any stage. When this consistency is reached, remove from the heat and allow to cool.

Place the zest and juice of the 3 oranges with the Grand Marnier in a pan and reduce by a half, when cool add to the crème anglaise.

Melt dark chocolate in bain marie, lightly whip double cream, combine egg yolks and sugar. Mix dark chocolate, cream and sabayon together, fold in slowly. Add brandy, place in a terrine, lined with clingfilm, to set.

Place orange custard on centre of the plate, chocolate terrine at the side, dust with cocoa powder and serve

Chris Taylor, Executive Head Chef
Botley Park Hotel and Country Club
Winchester Road, Boorley Green, Botley
Tel: 01489 789242

DESSERTS and PUDDINGS

Butlocks Heath School opened on the 1st February 1876. Within 6 weeks of the opening, the appointed Head mistress, Mrs Barbara Gothard, instigated the first cookery lesson which she took herself. The older girls in the school took part, and between them they prepared dinner for 36 children. The ingredients of this first meal are unknown but an entry in the School Log dated 3 May 1876 tells us that the girls cooked:
Potato pie, stewed beef with barley, rice pudding, cornflour pudding and sick room beverage – lemonade, linseed tea, apple and barley waters.

On the 10th July 1891 the cookery class made 90lbs of strawberry jam!

In August and September 1918 the children were given a total of 10 half days for the purpose of blackberry picking and at the end of that time, the combined effort of some 300 pupils had resulted in the astonishing total of 17cwt. 1 quart. 11lbs of blackberries being dispatched to 'the recognised jam factory'.

STIRRING TRADITIONS

Butlocks Pudding

8 oz (225g) suet
8 oz (225g) raisins
8 oz (225g) plain flour
Pinch salt
1 teaspoon nutmeg
1 egg
¼ pint (150ml) milk

Chop suet very finely, stone and cut raisins in half, mix together with the flour, also the salt and nutmeg. Beat the egg, add it to the milk and stir. Add the liquid to the dry ingredients and mix well together.

Tie the mixture up in a well-floured pudding cloth. Put the pudding in a saucepan of boiling water (with a small plate at the bottom of the saucepan to keep it from sticking) and boil for at least 3 hours.

 Unwrap the pudding and serve it hot with caster sugar sifted over the top or accompanied with a sweet white sauce.

This in an old recipe that would have originally been cooked on the kitchen range.

Botley High Street, 1907
courtesy of Botley and Curdridge Local History Society

About 200 years ago Botley Square was an area of turf and the market was held there. After a period of disuse the market was revived in 1830. On one occasion 1,280 sheep, 150 lambs, 250 cattle and 200 pigs were sold; each owner selling his own beasts. By tradition at the end of the market, farmers sat down to a meal which always included the Botley Plum pudding.

Botley Plum Pudding

½ lb (225g) suet
½ lb (225g) sugar
2 eggs, beaten
½ lb (225g) breadcrumbs
1 lb (450g) raisins
1 teacup full of plain flour
½ pint (300ml) of milk
1 teaspoon grated nutmeg

Mix all the ingredients together well and spoon into a lightly greased pudding basin. Closely wrap with a cloth and tie with string. Place in a suitable pan, pour boiling water to halfway up the basin, cover with a lid and boil for 3½ hours, topping up the water to ensure it does not boil dry.

Peach and Whisky Mousse

822g can peach slices
2 fl oz (60ml) peach wine
Splash Gale's whisky
4 tablespoons powdered gelatine
10 fl oz (300g) double cream
4 oz (115g) caster sugar

Drain the peaches, add the wine and whisky and purée in a blender until VERY smooth. Make up the gelatine as per the instructions and add to the peach puree. Whip the cream and caster sugar together until stiff then fold in the peach mixture. Spoon into glasses and chill 2 - 3 hours before serving.

Jon Daley, Gales Brewery

Wholemeal Fruit Cake

110g currants
110g sultanas or raisins
110g margarine
170g soft brown sugar
55g mixed peel, chopped
25g glacé cherries, chopped
225ml water
1 teaspoon bicarbonate of soda
1 teaspoon ground nutmeg
2 teaspoons mixed spice
225g wholemeal flour
1 teaspoon baking powder
Pinch of salt
2 eggs, lightly beaten

use more cherries to add extra colour to the cake

Wash the dried fruit and place in a saucepan with the margarine, sugar, peel, cherries, water, bicarbonate of soda and spices. Bring to the boil, reduce the heat and simmer gently for 1 minute. Pour into a large mixing bowl and allow to cool.

Preheat the oven to 180ºC/350ºF/Mark 4.

Lightly grease and line an 18cm square cake tin and lightly grease the lining paper.

Sift the flour with the baking powder and salt, returning any residue in the sieve to bowl with the sifted flour. Stir into the melted mixture together with the lightly beaten eggs. Mix well and place into the prepared tin, smoothing over the top.

Bake for 1 to 1½ hours or until golden in colour, firm to the touch and beginning to shrink from the tin sides.

Cool in the tin for 15 minutes before turning onto a cooling rack.

Traditionally served with apple and cheese.

From the Bursledon Windmill Recipe Book
Bursledon Windmill, Windmill Lane, Bursledon,
Tel: 023 8040 4999

Bursledon Windmill is Hampshire's only working windmill. It was built by Mrs Phoebe Langtry between 1813 and 1814 on the site of an earlier mill and was in use until the 1880's. Hampshire Buildings Preservation Trust restored the mill to its former glory between 1976 - 1991.

Now managed by the Hampshire County Council Museums Service, the mill again grinds wheat making stoneground flour much as it did in the 19th century.

The high quality flour from Bursledon Windmill is used by various Hampshire bakeries. You can call in whenever the sails are turning to buy your flour for home baking. The strong wholemeal flour is particularly good for bread baking and organic flour for scones, pastry and cakes.

Pumpkin Cookies

1 cup of caster sugar
½ cup butter
1 egg
1 cup pumpkin, cooked and puréed
1 teaspoon vanilla essence
1 teaspoon baking powder
1 teaspoon bicarbonate soda
2 cups plain flour
½ teaspoon salt
2 teaspoon cinnamon
1 cup chopped nuts
1 cup raisins

Preheat oven to 190ºC/375ºF/Mark 5.

Cream the sugar and butter together, and then add the egg, pumpkin and vanilla essence. Sift baking powder, bicarbonate, flour, salt and cinnamon and add to mixture. Add the nuts and raisins and mix well.

Prepare a standard baking tray/sheet and drop small spoonfuls of mixture onto the tray and cook in the oven for 12 – 15 minutes until golden brown.

Jubilee Sailing Trust

Nut and Apricot Fingers

8 oz (225g) dried apricots (no soak kind)
4 oz (115g) butter
2 oz (50g) caster sugar
5 oz (150g) plain flour
2 eggs
5 oz (150g) light soft brown sugar
½ teaspoon baking powder
2 oz (50g) flaked almonds

Preheat oven 180ºC/350ºF/Mark 4.

Chop apricots into small pieces and put in pan covered with cold water, poach for 15 minutes until they are soft. Drain off the liquid and set the apricots aside.

Grease and line a shallow 7½ inch square (19cm) tin. Mix the butter, caster sugar and 4 oz (115g) flour into a soft dough. Cover the base of the tin with this mixture and bake "blind" for 20 minutes.

In the meantime, beat the eggs and mix in the remaining flour, brown sugar and baking powder. Stir in the apricots and spread the mixture over the cooked base. Sprinkle the top with the flaked almonds. Place in the oven and bake for 25 minutes or until puffed and golden. Leave to cool before removing from tin. Peel off the paper and cut into fingers.

Botley Womens Institute

Mrs Dundas's Biscuits

Martha Lloyd was born in 1765, and was one of 3 children, one of whom, her youngest sister, Mary married James Austen in 1797.

In 1805 following the death of her mother, Martha moved in with Mrs George Austen, Cassandra and Jane and moved with them to Chawton Cottage. Throughout her life and time with the Austens, Martha made a collection of recipes both culinary and household. One of the recipes that was mentioned in her collection was a biscuit recipe from Mrs Dundas who was a friend of Martha's from Berkshire.

The original recipe:

Take 2 oz of lard or butter, & 2 lb of flour, mix them well together with a little cold water, work or knead them very well roll your biscuits very thin, & prick them exceedingly, bake them on tins in a very quick oven, looking constantly at them or they will scorch.

Modern version of Mrs Dundas's Biscuits:

½ oz (15g) [1 tablespoon] of butter
8 oz (225g) [2 cups] of flour
Good pinch of salt
1 fl oz (30ml) cold water

Makes 10 – 12 biscuits

Preheat the oven to 220ºC/435ºF /Mark 7; also grease and flour two baking trays lightly or cover with baking parchment.

Mix the butter into the flour with salt; in a food processor is the easiest way. When the mixture is like fine bread-crumbs, add a little cold water: you will need about 2 tablespoons altogether, but only add a little at a time and

CAKES and BAKES

work the liquid into the dry ingredients very thoroughly after each addition, until you have a stiff dough.

Roll out the dough as thinly as you possibly can, and cut into rounds with a 4 inch (10cm) cutter. Prick each one all over with a fork. Place the rounds on the prepared baking trays and put them straight into the oven, near the top. Look at them after 3 minutes, and thereafter keep a close eye on them until they begin to colour. Then remove and cool on a wire rack.

From The Jane Austen Cookbook
Courtesy of The British Museum Press

For nearly three hundred years, Netley Abbey was home to monks of the Cistercian Order founded at Citeaux (in Latin, Cistercium), Burgundy at the end of the Eleventh Century.

Cuthbert Monk 1886 *'At first the Cistercian rule as to fasting and religious exercises was exceedingly rigorous: they ate neither fish nor fowl, nor even eggs, butter, cheese they might eat only if given to them in aims; and they had only two meals a day besides mixtum which seems to have been an indifferent kind of porridge indeed. Every Friday in Lent they had but one less mess of this throughout the day. Broth not of a very good kind either was served out to them in a very small measure.'*

Poets and writers have been inspired by these old stones, Jane Austen and members of her family picnicked beneath the walls.

CAKES and BAKES

'We all except Grandmama, took a boat and went to Netley Abbey (sic) the ruins of which look beautiful. We ate some biscuits we had taken and returned home quite delighted'

Wrote Fanny Knight about an excursion with her Aunt Jane.

In the 18th Century whilst staying with Charles Mordaunt, the Earl of Peterborough, at his home at Bevis Mount, the poet Alexander Pope joined him on a boat trip down Southampton Water. With Peterborough at the helm they came ashore at Netley Abbey and had a picnic of "Cold Pye, Pig(e)ons, and Turkies" and wines supplied by French sailors. They ate sitting on fallen pillars.

The abundant fish supply was one of the main reasons for the location of Netley Abbey. In the 1900's vessels came to this area from as far as Cornwall. Their catches of crabs, lobsters and oysters were stored underwater in perforated boxes and then sent to Billingsgate Market.

Wholemeal Fruit Cake

See page 94

Celebration Day Apple Cake

1 lemon
1kg. Cox's apples (or other rich flavoured eating apple)
250g margarine
250g caster sugar
4 eggs
500g self-raising flour
10 tablespoons milk
2 handfuls sultanas
100g flaked almonds

> The most famous apple from Hampshire is probably the Hambledon Deux Ans, a long keeping dual-purpose apple that originated in Hambledon.

Preheat the oven to 170ºC/325ºF/Mark 3.

Squeeze the juice of the lemon into a mixing bowl. Peel core and chop the apples into 1 - 2cm chunks, don't chop too small. Do not use Bramley or other cooking apples since this will make the cake too soggy. Stir chopped apple into lemon juice until coated, and then add 2 handfuls of sultanas. Set this aside to rest and make the cake mix.

Cream margarine and caster sugar until smooth. Add the eggs one at a time beating in with a tablespoon of sieved self-raising flour to each egg. Fold in the remaining flour and the milk. Line a deep 14 x 10inch roasting dish with buttered greaseproof paper and put half the cake mixture into the dish. Cover with the apple and sultana mixture and top with remaining cake mix. Sprinkle the top thickly with flaked almonds.

Bake for 40 minutes. If still too soft in the centre reduce heat to 150ºC/300ºF/Mark 2 and cook for a further 15 minutes.

Cut into squares, serve hot or cold.

Stephen & Julia Hayes, Fruitwise

CAKES and BAKES

During the early 20th century strawberry growing was a major industry in the Botley and Hedge End area. June was the main strawberry picking month and it would involve the whole family. They would rise at 4am and began picking the crops soon afterwards filling the 3lb baskets they carried with them.

The strawberries were taken straight to Botley train station, where they were loaded onto the trains known as the 'strawberry specials' bound for London, Manchester, Cardiff and Glasgow, where the fresh strawberries were relished in the top hotels and restaurants. The first consignment of each day left Botley station at 8am.

Strawberry Pickers

Strawberry Shortcake

4 oz (115g) caster sugar
8 oz (225g) butter, softened
12 oz (350g) plain flour

Topping:

8 oz (225g) icing sugar
1 capful of pink food colouring
1 capful strawberry flavouring
8 oz (225g) plain cooking chocolate
16 fresh strawberries

Preheat the oven to 200ºC/400ºF/Mark 6.

Mix sugar, butter and flour together to make a stiff paste.
Press the paste into a lined baking tray and prick it all over
with a fork. Bake in the oven for about 20 - 25 minutes
until the shortbread is just starting to brown at edges.
Allow to cool.

Make up a fondant icing with icing sugar, colouring and
flavouring to make a stiff paste. Spread over the cooled
shortbread, adding more icing sugar if the fondant too soft.

Melt the chocolate in a bowl and dip the strawberries in
until half covered in chocolate and leave them to set on a
sheet of foil.

Pour remaining chocolate over the shortbread and spread
evenly. (It might need melting a little more after strawberry
dipping!) Decorate by placing the chocolate strawberries
onto the chocolate covered shortbread at regular intervals
before the chocolate sets.

Chris Pullen, Village Tea Rooms
Village Tea Rooms, High Street, Hamble
Tel: 023 8045 5583

CAKES and BAKES

Chestnut and Chocolate Cake

435g unsweetened chestnut purée
2 tablespoons honey
400g dark chocolate, minimum 70% cocoa solids
50g butter
400g gingernut biscuits
Glass of sweet sherry
50g icing sugar
Shredded coconut or nuts, strawberries and whipped cream
to decorate

Liberally grease a 30cm springform cake tin. Mix the chestnut purée with the honey and set aside. Melt the chocolate over a low heat with the butter and set aside. Briefly dip the biscuits in the sherry and line the cake tin with half the biscuits. Spread half the chestnut puree over the biscuits and drizzle a quarter of the chocolate over. Layer with the remainder of the biscuits and then the chestnut puree and a further quarter of the chocolate. Leave in the fridge for at least two hours.

 Just before serving, mix the remaining chocolate with the icing sugar and decorate the cake as desired.

This is a very rich cake and tastes gorgeous with ice cream.

Venika Kingsland

CAKES and BAKES

Mrs Wenman was instrumental in forming the cookery classes at Butlocks Heath School around 1890. She raised them to such a high standard that they were regarded as a model for all schools in the area to copy. In 1893, Mrs Wenman published an 'Elementary Schools Cookery Book', which deals with the reasons for teaching cookery details of the running of the class. So successful was the cookery curriculum that Her Majesty's Inspector recommended a great number of School Managers and teachers to come for advice to this, "the pioneer school of cookery" in the Southampton district.

Market Hall, Botley High Street

Cake a la Wenman

8 oz (225g) plain flour
4 oz (115g) ground rice
4 oz (115g) cornflour
4 oz (115g) dripping
8 oz (225g) raisins, stoned and halved
4 oz (115g) sugar
One teaspoon of baking powder
¼ teaspoon bicarbonate of soda
One egg
½ pint (300ml) milk
One teaspoon essence of lemon

Preheat the oven to 180ºC/350ºF/Mark 4.

Put flour, rice, cornflour and fat into a bowl, and rub the fat into the flour mix. Add the raisins, the sugar and the baking powder and mix well. Beat egg and mix the milk and the essence with it, adding it to the mixture making a stiff paste. Put it into a well-oiled tin and bake for one hour.

This cake improves by being kept a day or two.

Taken from the book
Butlocks Heath School Days 1876 – 1984

CAKES and BAKES

In the 17th century, cherry trees grew in abundance throughout the village and each year people came from surrounding places to buy cherries (or merries as they were called). The merrie is said to be a black and bitter cherry from Kent. None of those trees still growing seem to bear fruit. Captain Fortune published a book about 1960 in which he says that Merrie Festivals were held in Ramalley but ceased after much drunkenness and it seems that the flowers were of more importance than any berries.

Oliver Cromwell writes in the summer after the marriage of his son Richard to Dorothy (May Day 1649) that 'he is glad the young people have leisure to make a journey to eat cherries. There is little doubt but that this must have been to the gardens in Ram-Alley near Chandler's Ford .... where numerous trees, bearing quantities of little black cherries called merries, used to grow, and where parties used to go as a Sunday diversion, and eat, before the days of the station and the building'.

from John Kebles Parishes
by Charlotte Yonge

Merrie Cherrie Cheesecake Bars

⅓ cup cold butter
⅓ cup firmly packed brown sugar
1 cup all-purpose flour
8 oz (225g) cream cheese (at room temp.)
¼ cup sugar
1 egg
1 tbsp lemon juice
¼ cup green glacé cherries, chopped
¼ cup red glacé cherries, chopped

Makes
About 36 bars

Preheat oven to 180ºC/350ºF/Mark 4.

In a large mixing bowl, cut the butter in chunks and add the brown sugar and the flour using a hand mixer mix them together on a low speed. Then beat at medium speed, scraping sides of bowl often, until it is well mixed (for about 1 minute). Reserve about ½ cup of this crumb mixture for topping.

Press remaining mixture into an 8 inch square (20cm) baking tray and bake in centre of oven for 10-12 minutes.

Prepare the filling while the base bakes. In a bowl, beat the cream cheese, sugar, egg and lemon juice together at medium speed until fluffy (for 1-2 minutes). Stir in the chopped cherries.

Spread the filling over part-cooked base and sprinkle the top with remaining crumb mixture. Return the baking tray to the oven and continue baking for a further 18-20 minutes or until filling is set and the top is lightly browned. Cool and store in refrigerator.

Andy Milner
Chandlers Ford and Hiltingbury Local Area Co-ordinator.

CAKES and BAKES

Farmworkers from Hiltonbury Farm lived in the cottages and would brew the beer for the Merrie Feasts in the cottages; Richard Cromwell visited in the late 1600's when he lived at Hursley Park House having married the daughter of the owner.

This photo was taken in the early 20th century when the Betteridge family lived there (you can just about make out Mrs Betteridge in the photo). The cottages were demolished in the 20th century and is now the site of the Scout Hut.

Barbara Hillier

This picture is of a 17th century cottage at Ramalley, one of a group of 7 cottages.

Merrie Cherrie Chocolate Muffins

8 oz (225g) Philadelphia cheese
16 oz (450g) confectioner's sugar
6 oz (175g) Maraschino cherries, drained
2 cups pecan nuts, halved
24 prepared chocolate muffins (2½ inch deep)

In medium bowl, with an electric mixer, beat the cream cheese until smooth. Slowly add confectioner's sugar, beating until smooth and creamy.

Reserve 12 whole cherries; coarsely chop remaining cherries. Reserve 1 cup of the pecan halves (about 72) and roughly chop the rest.

In a small bowl, combine ¾ of the cream cheese frosting, chopped pecans and chopped cherries. Using the end of a wooden spoon, poke a 1 inch deep hole in the top of each muffin. Spoon about 1 tablespoonful pecan filling in each hole. Frost the tops of the muffins with the remaining frosting.

Halve reserved cherries. Top muffins with cherry halves and reserved pecan halves. Refrigerate the cakes until ready to serve.

Makes 24 cakes

Andy Milner
Chandlers Ford and Hiltingbury Local Area Co-ordinator.

Botley Mills and Carters in 1900

This recipe was originally created using flour from Botley Mills.

However, flour is no longer milled at Botley.

According to the Domesday Book, there were two mills in Botley worth 20 shillings; at least one of these is thought to have been more upstream at the end of the tidal River Hamble. The Duke of Portland owned the mill from 1536 until 1775. The oldest part still standing was built in 1770 and is a three-storey brick building of 7 bays and a tiled roof.

Date and Orange Cake

4 tablespoons orange juice
Grated rind of 1 orange
4 tablespoons (4oz) [115g] golden syrup
3 oz (85g) soft brown sugar
2 tablespoons water
6 fl oz (175ml) vegetable oil
2 standard eggs
8 oz (225g) wholemeal or wheatmeal flour
2 teaspoons baking powder
Pinch of salt
6 oz (175g) dates, well chopped
extra sugar
7 inch (18 cm) cake tin, lined and greased

Preheat oven to 170ºC/325ºF/Mark 3.

In a bowl, put the orange juice and rind, golden syrup, sugar, water, vegetable oil, beaten eggs and half of the flour, mix together and beat for 1 – 2 minutes. Stir in rest of the flour, baking powder, salt and the dates.

Put the cake mix in the prepared tin and sprinkle the top with extra sugar and bake for 1¼ - 1½ hours.

Keep for several days to improve the flavour.

Botley Mills,
Botley, Southampton,
Tel: 01489 782202

CAKES and BAKES

In July 1981 Mrs. Kathleen Trott, a stalwart member of Hamble W.I., called a meeting of interested people, with a view to opening a W.I. Market in the village of Hamble. Producers paid 5p. to become shareholders; a Committee was formed with Mrs. Trott as Chairman and her husband Alan as Treasurer.

The market opened on Friday 18th September 1981 at 10am as affiliated members of Hampshire W.I. Markets Ltd. in the Hamble Memorial Hall. One stall sold all the home-baked goods, jams and eggs, another stall was laden with home grown vegetables, plants and flowers, and the third stall had a fine selection of craft items. Business was good each week. We also took part at outside events such as The Village Carnivals, Open Days and the Hampshire Show in the Victoria Country Park.

By 1994 the contributions that had to be paid to Hampshire W.I. Markets Ltd. were mounting and compared to other larger markets in Hampshire we were finding it hard to meet the spiralling costs.

A meeting of Shareholders was called and it was decided to leave Hampshire W.I. Markets and trade independently. On January 1st 1995 Hamble Village Market was inaugurated and on Friday 6th January 1995 we held our first market in Hamble Memorial Hall. We still attend occasional Outside Events and since 2001 we have made and sold hundreds of Mince Pies at the annual Victorian Christmas Market at the Royal Victoria Country Park at Netley.

STIRRING TRADITIONS

Oat Crunchies

9 oz (250g) oats
5 oz (150g) demerara sugar
6½ oz (190g) Olivio, melted

Preheat the oven to 220ºC/425ºF/Mark 7.

Mix all the ingredients together well and spread the mixture into a baking tray 9 inch square (23 cm). Bake in the hot oven for 5 - 7 minutes.

Mark into squares while still hot, but allow to cool before removing the crunchies from tin.

Beryl Meigh of the Hamble Village Market
Hamble Village Market, Memorial Hall,
Every Friday, 10am – 11am

HSB, Onion and Dill Bread

Use a standard white bread mix but replace some of the water with HSB (you can drink the rest!!), then simply add chopped dill and some onion powder when making.

Jon Daley, Gales Brewery

CAKES and BAKES

Wassail is an Anglo-Saxon greeting meaning "good health" or "I wish you well". By the twelfth century, it had become the salutation you offered as a toast, to which the standard reply was to hail, "drink good health".

In Southern England a set of customs was grouped under the name of wassailing. They consisted, in essence, of wishing health to crops and animals much as people passing the wassail bowl wished it to each other. The toasting of good health of apple trees was originally a tradition that took place on Twelfth Night, so that the apple trees would bear the crop from which next years cider would be made. Fruitwise hold their wassail on the second Saturday of the New Year, they have a bonfire, song, Morris Dancers and food is put in the trees for the robins and thanksgiving is made for the old year's crop.

"Old Apple tree, we wassail thee, and hope that thou shalt bear
For the Lord does know where we shall be when apples come
                                        again next year
For to bear well, and to bloom well, how happy we shall be
Let every man take off his cap and shout to the old apple tree

Old apple tree we wassail thee, and hope that thou shalt bear
Hats full, caps full, shell bags and buckets full
And a little heap under the stair"

A Christmas recipe-

> Add to your meal some merriment
> And a thought for kith and kin
> And then as a prime ingredient
> A plenty of wit thrown in
> But spice it all with the essence of love
> And a little whiff of play
> Let wise old book and a glance above
> Complete a well-spent day

Gordon Cox, Eastleigh and District Local History Society

STIRRING TRADITIONS

Wassail Bowl

1 cinnamon stick
4 cloves
1 allspice, crushed
1 orange, chopped
1 pinch nutmeg
1 star anise
1 pint (600ml) apple juice
3 pints (1.8 litres) strong dry cider

Simmer the stick of cinnamon with the cloves, allspice, the orange pieces, the nutmeg and a piece of star anise (the spices can be varied to suit ones taste) in a pint of apple juice for half and hour. Add 3 pints of strong dry cider, preferably still (if fizzy cider is used it may froth over so add it slowly). Serve hot, not boiling, in stone or pewter mugs, preferably around a bonfire in the orchard.

Stephen & Julia Hayes, Fruitwise

Victorian Wassailers

Hampshire fare is Hampshire's local food group and represents and promotes the interests of food, drink and rural craft businesses based in the county.

The organisation offers marketing services to producers and acts as a central point of reference to the public, trade and media. For further information or a free guide to producers, please telephone **01962 845999** or visit www.hampshirefare.co.uk

Please find listed below a list of the local producers in and around the Hamble Valley where you can purchase your ingredients to create the new and traditional recipes from this book.

Charles Baynham Butcher and Food Emporium
20 Bournemouth Road, ChandlersFord (butcher),
87-93 Hiltingbury Road, Chandlers Ford (emporium)
Telephone: **023 8025 2019** (butcher)
Telephone: **023 8025 3004** (emporium)

High class traditional family butcher plus grocery lines and wines. South African foods a speciality, including biltong and boerewors. Open: Monday-Saturday 7am-5pm

Bursledon Windmill
Bursledon Windmill, Windmill Lane, Bursledon.
Just off J8 M27
Telephone: **023 8040 4999**

Explore Hampshire's only working windmill and purchase flour for baking at home, including strong wholemeal flour ideal for bread-making and organic flour ideal for scones, pastry and cakes.
Open: 10am-4pm and whenever the sails are turning.

Fruitwise
Telephone: **01489 796790**   www.fruitwise.co.uk
(Please refer to website for diary of sales and events where produce can be purchased).

Fruit and vegetable gardens and orchards producing rare/old English varieties of apples selected for flavour, ripened naturally and sold in season (July-January). Organically grown soft fruit and vegetables. Jams, chutneys, jellies, marmalade and fruit curd available all year. Free tastings are usually available.

George Gale and Co. Ltd
The Hampshre Brewery, Horndean
Telephone: **023 9271 4484** Website: www.gales.co.uk

Independent family brewery established 1847, award winning beers including HSB and Prize Old Ale, over 100 pubs in the area. Brewery Shop open: Mon – Fri 10.00am – 5.00pm, Saturday 10.00am – 2.00pm

A & Margaret Johnson, Honey and Hive Products
Grasmead, Limekiln Lane, Dean, Bishops Waltham, Southampton, SO32 1FY
Telephone: **01489 892390** www.hampshirefare.co.uk/johnson

Beekeepers producing local honeys, honey marmalade and five different honey mustards, chutneys and heather honey fudge using home produced honey to sweeten. Available in Hampshire retail outlets, from the door and mail order.

Lewry's Traditional Butcher
Nick Hillier, 20 High Street, Botley.
Telephone: **01489 782 019**

Traditional butcher selling a wide range of local, naturally produced meats. Homemade sausages and burgers a speciality. Shop also sells other Hampshire Fare products. Open: Tuesday-Thursday 8am-5pm, Friday till 6pm, Saturday 8am-2pm

R Owton Butcher & Chalcroft Farm Shop
Chalcroft Farm, Burnetts Lane, West End,
Southampton, SO30 2HU
Telephone: **023 8069 2206**

Traditional family butcher, where the finest quality, warm friendly service and a real value commitment to value for money are their main objectives. Wide range of home made sausages, 2002 supreme champion of Hampshire for their sausages.
Open: 7am - 5pm Monday - Friday, 7am - 4pm Saturday

Pickwell Farm Shop
Pickwell Farm, Portsmouth/Grange Road, Netley
Telephone: **023 8040 4616**

32 varieties of vegetables and fruit, plus cut flowers, bedding plants and hanging baskets. PYO and farm shop. Open every day 9am-5pm

L. J. Smith Family Butchers

3 Riverside, Bishopstoke, Eastleigh, SO50 6LP
Telephone: **023 8064 4040**

Award winning sausage producer with over 75 varieties available.
Also free range pork, cheeses and home made pies. 2003 winner of
the Hampshire sausage competition! Open: Monday-Wednesday
7am-5.30pm, Thursday-Friday 6am-6pm, Saturday 6am-4pm

The Watercress Company Ltd

Contact: Mr C. Barter The Nythe, Alresford
Telephone: **01962 734084**

Producing watercress and salads for UK multiples.

Wickham Vineyard

Botley Road, Shedfield, Hampshire
Telephone: **01329 834042**
www.wickhamvineyard.co.uk

Set in beautiful countryside. Highly praised audio-tour takes you
around the vineyard and high tech winery, explaining the wine-
making process and includes a wine tasting afterwards in the wine
and gift shop. Wander through the vineyard on a self-guided tour.
Open 10.30am - 5.30pm Monday-Saturday, 11.30am - 5 pm Sunday

Stock up your cupboards with local produce and ingredients from the many local suppliers and markets.

HAMPSHIRE
FARMERS' MARKETS LTD

Hampshire Farmers' Markets were set up to give local farmers and growers the opportunity to sell directly to the public.

The markets also allow customers the opportunity to talk with the producers, try produce before they buy, discuss how the product was grown, raised or baked and also get recipe suggestions and tips on how to best cook the products on offer. All the produce must come from Hampshire or within ten miles of the border. There are an average of 45 stallholders attending each market and this ensures that there is always a wide range of produce including free range beef, pork, lamb and chicken, rare breed meat, oven-ready game, fresh fish and crabs from the Solent, fresh and smoked trout and even ostrich and water buffalo! Seasonal fruit and vegetables are plentiful and there is always organic produce, freshly baked bread, a variety of cheeses, wines, jams, honeys, cakes and much more.

For further information on Hampshire Farmers' Markets
please call **01962 845135**
or look at their website:-
www.hampshirefarmersmarkets.co.uk

Hampshire County Council working to support local food initiatives in the county.

Conversion Tables

Weights		Volume		Measure	
1 oz	25g	½ fl.oz	15ml	¼ inch	0.5cm
2	50	1	30	½	1
3	80	2	60	1	2.5
4	115	3	90	2	5
5	150	4	125	3	7.5
6	175	5 (¼ pt)	150	4	10
7	200	10	300	5	13
8	225	15	450	6	15
9	250	1 pt	600	7	18
10	275	1¼ pt	725	8	20
12	350	1½ pt	850	9	23
14	400	1¾ pt	1 litre	10	25
16 (1lb)	450	2 pt	1.15 ltr	11	28
1½ lb	750	3 pt	1.75 ltr	12	30.5

Gas	Oven Temperature	
Mark 1	140ºC	275ºF
2	150	300
3	170	325
4	180	350
5	190	375
6	200	400
7	220	425
8	230	450
9	240	475

Other	Measures
5 ml	teaspoon
15 ml	tablespoon
250 ml	1 cup

Index

Chestnut soup	19
Chicken, curried	39
Chicken mozzarella melts	41
Chicken, spring thyme	59
Chilli chicken nests	42
Chocolate muffins, merrie cherrie	111
Chocolate terrine, dark, with orange custard	89
Coconut and GB beer batter prawns	31
Cookies, pumpkin	96
Corned beef hash	45
Cream of watercress soup	25
Curried chicken	39
Custard, orange	89

D

Dark chocolate terrine with orange custard	89
Date and orange cake	113

E

Escalope of veal in breadcrumbs	65

F

Farmer's pastry	63
Fish bake	33
Fish pie with cherry sauce	34
Fruit cake, wholemeal	94

G

GB beer, and coconut, battered prawn	31
Ginger and butternut squash risotto	77
Gooseberry meringue	86

H

Hamble Valley venison with white beans and bacon	60
Hampshire sausages	57
Hash, corned beef	45
Hikers' delight	86
Honey dressing	17